Bound
by
Choices

LaKisha Avery-Stewart

ISBN 978-1-64079-094-0 (Paperback)
ISBN 978-1-64079-095-7 (Digital)

Christian Faith Publishing, Inc.
296 Chestnut Street
Meadville, PA 16335
www.christianfaithpublishing.com

Printed in the United States of America

Acknowledgments

Giving all praises to our Heavenly Father for without Him I wouldn't be here today. I thank you Lord for loving me and being patient with me throughout the many choices that I've made in my life. I also like to thank you, Lord, for protecting me and choosing me to be an instrument for your people. Please continue to have mercy on me and surround me with your presence.

I want to thank my loving husband Jeffery for being patient with me and keeping the kids occupied when I was glued to the computer typing this novel. And for all the support and encouragement that he provided throughout this whole process.

I'm so thankful for my loving kids Destin, Jayden, Khloe and Jazmine for motivating me and for being understanding on the days I didn't cook and it was every man for himself.

To my mom and dad for the strength and power that each of you possess and the love and guidance you provided. Mom, thank you for your support and hospitality toward my family and me, and for the best birthday gift a daughter could ever receive. I love you, Mom.

To my siblings and cousins who continue to give me the love and support that I need and for the helpful ideas that you provided. I love you and appreciate everything you did.

To my grandmothers, Ella and Lola, thank you for being the strong black women that you are and wonderful role models, not only to me but to all the kids that you've helped raised.

Thank you, Granny Lola and twin Lawonda, for taking out the time and reading the book and providing me with constructive criticism.

To everyone else who supported me I love you and thank you for being who you are. And for those who didn't believe thank you for being who you are and always remember it's not up to you to believe but it's up to the one with the vision to believe.

Love You All.

Contents

Preface

For God only knows when and how your journey is going to end and it's up to you to live through the plan. Have you made the right choices in your life or are you still behind time holding on to things that you should have let go.

We determine how hard or easy the road is going to be by the choices that we make. Why is it so hard to make the right choice but so easy to do wrong? A person once said to me, "Everything that looks good on the outside isn't good on the inside and everything that comes easy to you isn't good for you."

Have you been choosing the path that seems easy or have you been choosing the path that requires a lot of time and hard work?

I'm here to tell you that God is looking for some hard workers to be about His business. There are so many lost souls out there that are crying out and to them it seems as if no one is listening.

Change

Jewels

The sun is shining and I can hear the wind blowing as I lay comfortably in my bed. A smile races across my face as I begin to think about the fun that I had with my dad on this morning. For the first time, in a long time, I felt the connection. It had been a long time since he had taken time out with me, and this morning was special. You see my daddy is a businessman who travels often, so I never really get to see him because his company is always sending him on business trips. I had a funny feeling that something was going to change today, but I wasn't quite sure of what it would be.

A loud noise was coming from the living room. I jumped up from my bed and walked down the hallway to get a closer look. As I came closer to the living room, I could hear the voices of my parents. My mother was saying words to my dad that I had never heard her say before. My heart started to beat fast and tears began to well up in my eyes. Why is my mom speaking to my dad this way? Was she mad at him because we hung out together? I hope I didn't cause any confusion. As my mom picked up the vase to throw it at my dad, I let out a loud scream. I couldn't stop screaming, so I ran into my room and fell onto my bed.

Why is this happening to me? Why are they fighting? My mom knocked on the door and walked in. She said, "Baby, I'm so sorry that you had to see your dad and me fussing."

I jumped up and said, "Why, why are you treating Daddy like this? Why are you trying to hurt him? I saw you pick up that vase.

You were going to throw it at him. We had a good time this morning and now you're mad." I stood up, looked into my mom's eyes, and said, "I hate you," and then I ran out of the room.

I ran in search of my dad, but he was nowhere to be found. I started to scream out, "Daddy, Daddy, please, Daddy, come here, I want to see you!" I ran back into my room and my mom was sitting there with tears streaming down her eyes. I started screaming, "How could you make him leave? What did you say to him? Why did you do this to me?" She didn't say a word. Tears just kept flowing down her face. I fell to the floor and began to cry again. This is not the change that I was looking for, and this can't be the change that's going to happen.

I woke up in the middle of the night looking for my father. I went into their room and noticed my mom was lying on the floor. I ran to her side and tried to wake her. When I turned her over, I noticed that her breath smelled like alcohol. I ran and called my dad. As the phone begins to ring, I continued to scream, "Momma! Get up, Momma! Momma, please get up! I don't hate you. I'm so sorry that I said that." He picked up the phone and I yelled, "Daddy, I think Mom is dead."

He asked, "Baby, what are you talking about?"

I began to tell him that she was lying on the floor and she smelled like alcohol and wouldn't get up. He told me he was on his way and that I needed to hang up the phone and dial 911. As the 911 operator answered, I began to scream again. "I think my mom is dead. Please come and help her!" The operator kept asking me all these questions I was so nervous I didn't know what to say. I heard my daddy's voice, "Angel, where are you?" I dropped the phone, "Daddy, I'm in your room! Please, Daddy, come here!" He ran into the room. He asked me if I called the operator and I told him that they were still on the line. He picked up the phone and began talking to the lady. He told her everything that she needed to know. I kept holding my momma and rocking her. I heard the sirens coming and before I knew it the men in the ambulance came running through the door.

"Is she dead?" I asked. The men didn't say a word. They just kept tending to my mother. They put her on a gurney and carried her out. I grabbed my dad's hand as tears ran down my face I asked my daddy if my mother was going to be okay.

He just looked at me and said, "Jewels, I really don't know."

We got into the car and followed the ambulance to the hospital. As we rode in silence, I thought about the events that had taken place earlier that day and asked my dad why he had left. He stated that he and my mother had a disagreement, but not to worry because everything was going be okay between the two of them. As I stared out the window at the beautiful palm trees of Los Angeles, a sense of peace came across my body after hearing my daddy say those words.

Cocaine

Mike

I can't believe this is happening. Why would my wife want to hurt herself? I paced back and forth thinking about the argument that took place last night. Was she mad because she didn't want to move? It has to be more to it than that.

The doctor walked up to me and said, "Your wife almost overdosed on cocaine and alcohol. The ambulance got there just in time. We want to keep her here overnight for observation."

I couldn't believe what the doctor was saying to me. *Cocaine,* I thought, *when did she start doing cocaine? How could I have not known? I wonder if Jewels knows.*

I told Jewels to come on so that we could go home. Jewels looked at me and said, "Is everything all right, Daddy?" I told her yes everything was fine and that her mother had to stay overnight for observation. "I'm glad you're home," Jewels said.

I looked at her and said, "Me too."

I kept thinking about the incidents that had occurred throughout the past couple of months as I drove down the dark highways of Los Angeles. I still couldn't understand why she would do something like this.

As I pulled into the garage, so many crazy things were going through my head. Jewels and I got out of the car and went into her room. We sat down and talked about what had happened. She asked me what the doctor had said, and I told her that her mom was going through some changes in her life and felt that alcohol was her way out. Jewels looked at me and said, "Daddy, you don't have to lie to me. I know Momma is doing drugs."

My eyes got real big as I looked at her and said, "What, you knew? Why didn't you tell me?" I asked.

She looked at me with fear in her eyes and said, "Momma told me not to. She said that if I did you would leave and I would never see you again."

I couldn't believe what I was hearing. My thirteen-year-old daughter has been keeping this from me for I don't know how long. I looked at her and said, "You don't ever have to worry about me leaving you. You're my angel and I will always be a part of your life."

I gave her a hug and kissed her good night. I walked in my room with pain going through my body. I always thought if I worked hard enough and kept a roof over my family's head everything would be okay.

I started looking through her things and to be honest I wanted to know what was going on, but I was scared of what I would find. I stopped looking and lay down on the bed. As I moved the covers, I saw an opened tube and a mirror. I picked up the tube, looked inside and sure enough there it was, a little residue of cocaine. I closed my eyes in disbelief wondering if it was because of me that she decided to take this route.

Turning Point

Jewels

I know my daddy is wondering how long my mom has been doing drugs. I was around the age of eleven when it all started, two years after my dad had gotten his new job. At first, we were all excited. He told us that we would be moving to the mountains. He took us shopping, bought my mom the Mercedes-Benz she always wanted, and in addition to that I got every name-brand item that you could ever think of. At the age of eleven, I was living like a movie star.

Our house sits on the mountains overlooking the beautiful ocean; five bedrooms with a movie room, inside pool, and a game room. My bedroom has a built-in study, a walk-in closet, and bathroom with a Jacuzzi in it. My mom and I were happy, and I had never seen my mom smile so much.

My dad's job started sending him on business trips. The time that I use to spend with him was cut short. First, he would be gone for weeks at a time and then it turned into months. At one point he was gone for three months. During those times he would fly back for the weekend. It was never the same. Every time he came back Momma would always find something to argue with him about.

I never could understand why she would be so angry at him all the time. He was so sweet about it and he would just sit there and let her vent. I think what she was saying was going in one ear and out the other.

My mom started to get bored around the house. She had everything she wanted and needed, but there was nothing else for her to do. One day she decided to go out with one of her friends. I was twelve at the time. I was so surprised that she had left me at home by myself. I was a little scared but I didn't tell her. I knew if my dad had found out, he would be very upset.

The next day, I woke up and my mother was nowhere to be found. I didn't know what to do. I wanted to call my dad, but I knew it would only start another argument. I walked into the kitchen to fix me a bowl of cereal and I heard a knock at the door. I looked through the peephole and there, my mom was lying on the ground. I opened the door as quickly as I could and pulled her inside. She was out of it for about four hours. I didn't know what to do or think.

That day was the beginning of hell for me. My mom's attitude changed, her actions toward me were very strange, and going out started to be a regular thing for her. I kept to myself, because if I didn't she would only find something to fuss at me about.

It amazed me how well she could put on an act when my dad returned home from his trips. It was like nothing had changed. She went back to being the old mom that I had always known. This was very creepy to me. I didn't know that someone could have more than one personality.

One day I walked into her room as she was sitting at her vanity. She turned to look at me and I had noticed that she had powder on her nose. She tried to play it off saying her nose looked shiny, so she put powder on it. The look she gave me was a look of fear and shame.

The incident didn't sit well with me so I decided to be nosey and go through her things one day while she was gone. I didn't find anything at first, but I couldn't stop as my curiosity took over and I began looking every place I thought to hide things that I didn't want to be found. I paced back and forth in her room thinking, *The drawer, no that's too easy, under the bed, no to easy. Under the mattress, no we flip that over every three months.* And then it hit me, *Her collection of books.*

My mom collects Terry McMillan books and she is a huge fan of hers. She kept those in an unreachable place. I remember getting a good spanking one day for playing with one of her books that she had started reading. I think I was about five then. She looked at me and said, "If you ever touch another one of my books your spanking is going to be a lot worse."

I grabbed one of them and began to flip through it. I noticed a couple of small empty packages. I grab another one and I found the same. I didn't understand it at first until a letter fell out one of the books. At first, I put it back and then my curiosity once again sat in. I opened the letter up slowly and it read:

Tracie,

Daddy was missing you. I knew you would contact me again. I hope to see you soon. I need a main lady and by the way you were looking that night I think you're the one. Let me know if you run out of cocaine. You know daddy always got what you need.

Love Daddy

I didn't understand what the letter was saying at first. I got on the Internet and looked up the word "cocaine" and that's when I found out cocaine was a drug. I couldn't believe my mother was on drugs. All my life she would say, "Don't do drugs, drugs are bad for you," and now I find out that for the last year she's been doing the same thing she told me not to do.

Now I know why she has been so angry all the time. I bet it's because of the drugs that her love toward me seems to grow so distant. I started going to parties and hanging out with my friends more. I was twelve years old going to high school parties. The guys there were fine and they drew to me. They made me feel good inside, like I was important. Not knowing that it was all a game, I met this guy by the name of Troy. I think he was sixteen at the time. I told him that I was fourteen. We hung out for about six months and then he started to get physical. He would say things like, "If you love me, then you would show me."

I was strong at first but then I started to get weak. It was like my hormones were calling out to him. He touched me in ways that I never been touched before and it felt good. I started having dreams about different ways he could make me feel good. It was crazy, but I liked it. It was as if he was in my mind or something.

My mom went out one night and he came over to the house. I was scared at first but he gave me something to drink and I started to feel relaxed. He kissed me on my neck and it felt good. I thought I was in love. I took him into my room and he began to take off my clothes. The way he touched me made me feel like I was in heaven. He whispered the words "I love you" into my ear and I just melted into his arms.

Then he stuck his penis in me and the pain that I felt was very new and I knew what I was doing wasn't right. I told him to get up and he wouldn't. It was as if he couldn't hear me. I kept saying, "Stop, move," but he didn't. I laid there in pain for hours it seemed but it was only for about three minutes. When he got off of me, I rolled over with tears in my eyes.

He said, "Not bad for a virgin, but I've had better." He began putting on his clothes and when he got ready to leave he looked at me and said, "See you around. I'll call you, don't call me." I gave him a funny look and he walk out of the door.

I ran to my bathroom crying. I turned on the shower and ran the water. I couldn't believe this was happening to me. I really thought he cared for me, but he only wanted to get in me. Sad to say, I never saw or heard from him again.

My mother was getting worse by the minute. My dad came home for my thirteenth birthday. He took a week's vacation and took my mom and I to Paris for my birthday. I always wanted to go. My dad always knew what I wanted. He took me to the museum and taught me a lot about the history of the arts. We went on a boat tour and the parks and gardens were so beautiful and different from Los Angeles. My mom was acting very distant. She didn't look so well either.

When we arrived back home, my dad took me shopping for my birthday. We had a lot of fun. At that time, I told him how lonely I was without him and how I wish he would come back home. He told me that his contract was almost up and that he should return home to stay real soon. I was so happy to hear that. I wanted to tell him what was going on with momma but I knew that would only make her upset, so I just enjoyed the time that we were having together.

I ran in the house to show momma what Dad had bought, but she wasn't there. I knew she was out getting more drugs. I just prayed that she didn't come home too late. About an hour later, she came back with dinner. She put on a big act in front of dad. We sat down at the table and talked about old times. I was enjoying the three of us being together, but in the back of my mind I knew that he would be leaving me again shortly. My heart started feeling sad knowing that once he left my mom will go back to her old ways.

That next morning after my dad left, my mom came into my room and started asking me questions about my father and me. I knew she was wondering if I told him anything. I got up and showed her the stuff he had gotten me and told her about the different stores he had taken me to. I told her that his contract was going to be up in another six months and that he would be returning home to stay. I could tell by the look in her eyes that she wasn't happy to hear that.

Dad and I went to Tiffany's and we picked out a beautiful bracelet for her. I asked her if she liked it and she smiled and said, "Yes." I never saw her wear it though.

Summer was almost here and that meant school was almost over. I was happy because I knew my dad would be home to stay. My mom and I became very distant. It was as if she was jealous of me. She started speaking negative toward me and saying that I was a daddy's girl.

My mind was getting confused because I never knew that my own mother could become jealous of me. I was finally getting over the incident with Troy and then it happened. One day I came home early from school and my mom had this man over to the house. I was thinking, *Dang my mom is mighty bold.*

The man looked at my mother and said, "Diamond, who we have here?" *Who is Diamond?* I thought, *My mom's name is Tracie.*

She said, "Daddy, this is my daughter."

I know she just didn't say daddy, I thought.

This so-called "Daddy guy" said, "I didn't know you had a daughter. Are you going to recruit her to the stable?"

My mom said, "No, Daddy, she's not stable material."

My mind was going up and down. Here I am, thirteen years old and I find out that my mother is a hooker. I just shook my head.

The man Daddy grabbed me and started looking me up and down. Then he said, "Diamond, she looks like she's stable material, let me see for myself."

I looked at him and said, "You better get your hands off of me." Before I knew it I was lying on the ground. This man just slapped me so hard across the face that my lip began to bleed.

I began to cry out to my mother. "Momma, are you going to let him do this to me?"

She just looked at me and said, "Baby, it will be okay, it won't hurt."

Tears started falling down my face. I couldn't believe that my own mother was going to sit here and watch this man rape me.

As he began to pull down my pants I cried out to my daddy. I cried, "Daddy, come save me. Please help me."

He looked at me and said, "That's right, call out my name."

I couldn't believe it. He stuck his penis in me so hard that pain went down my back. At that moment I began to vomit. I threw up all in his face.

He jumped up off me and said, "You nasty little B." He turned and looked at my mom and said, "Diamond, you were right, she's not stable material." Then he began to pee on me.

My momma ran up to him and said, "Daddy, I told you." She looked at me and gave me an evil look. I just laid there in disbelief.

When she walked him out the door I got up and ran into my room. I locked myself in my bathroom and got into the shower. I couldn't stop myself from crying.

Not only is my mother a junkie, but she is also a hooker. My vagina was in so much pain. As I stood there letting the water run down my body I noticed blood was coming from my vagina. I began screaming with hate in me. Trying to figure out what I had done to deserve this.

My mom knocks on the bathroom door and said, "This is our little secret and your daddy doesn't need to know anything about this." I began to cry hard as I slid down into the tub. I stayed in the bathroom for about two hours. The blood didn't stop so I put on a maxi pad hoping that this was just the beginning of my menstrual cycle. When I came out of the bathroom I locked the door to my bedroom and lay across my bed until I fell asleep.

My feelings toward my mother had changed. Hate for her began to grow in me more and more each day. We didn't talk much. She went her way and I went mine. I was counting down the months for the day that my dad would return. I wanted to call him and tell him what had happened, but I didn't because I knew it would hurt him. More so, I was afraid of what he might do to her.

I started to feel sorry for her because she started to look real bad in health. I was wondering how she would pull this one off when my dad returned home.

It was the day before my dad was to come home for good and she was not ready. She called the cleaning crew to come and clean the house. She went to the spa so they could put her back together. It was kind of funny watching her run around like a chicken with its head cut off. I just sat in my room and watched TV.

She would come in there from time to time asking me if I needed anything or if I wanted to hang out with her.

I couldn't believe it, for the last three months, she didn't say anything to me and the day before my dad returns, she wants to pretend as if nothing has happened. I just looked at her as if she was crazy and turned back around to watch TV.

That night while I was in bed, I heard voices. I was praying that it wasn't my mom's pimp. When I turned around to face the door to my bedroom I saw this tall handsome man standing at the door. I knew it was my father. I jumped out of my bed and into his arms.

I was so happy to see him. He lay in the bed with me and we started to talk. He asked me how school was and the things that I was doing while he was gone. He asked if I had a boyfriend. I told him a little bit about Troy and that after him, I really wanted to get to know myself more. He told me that he had plans for mom and me on tomorrow. He kissed me on my forehead and tucked me in. I asked him if he'd stay until I fell asleep and he said okay.

That next morning I woke up smelling pancakes and eggs. I knew that my dad was here and that last night wasn't a dream. He knew how much I loved his pancakes and eggs. I ran into the kitchen and there he was. I felt safe when my dad was around. I fixed us some orange juice and we sat down and talked. He asked me about momma and how our relationship was. I didn't know what to say, so I told him we were cool. He then asked how long she had been sleeping this late. I lied and told him for a couple of weeks, knowing that she's been doing it for almost a year and a half. We ate our breakfast and we left. He took me riding and he started talking to me about boys and the things that I needed to watch out for. I thought, *If you had only told me this a few months ago*. He took me to the park and we lay in the grass and looked at the sky. He then began to tell me about life and its many challenges. He shared with me some of his experiences with drugs and alcohol.

I wanted to tell him about momma so bad, but I couldn't. He told me if it wasn't for me he didn't think he would be where he is today. He said when I was born it opened his eyes and at that moment he began to change his life. He sought out help for the drugs and alcohol and he was so sad because he had to be away from me for a few months.

He told me that he felt bad for not being around like a father should be, but he knew it was going to help the family. He asked me if I would mind moving. I asked him where, and he said, "To Dallas."

I asked, "Why Dallas?"

He then told me that if we didn't want to move he would have to be away from us for another year. The company that he works for is starting up another company in Dallas and they've asked him to be the CEO.

I started thinking about all the things that I've gone through and I told him yes, I think it's time for a change. He gave me a big hug and said, "Angel, I love you." He then asked me what I thought my mother would say and then my heart dropped.

I thought, *Another argument is about to happen*. I looked at him and said, "I don't know, she might be ready for a change as well."

We went to the movies and then to the store to get some groceries. I can't remember the last time my mom and I went to the grocery store. We would eat out every day unless dad was coming home. We got home and she was sitting on the couch. I could tell she was mad. She looked at us and said, "I see you two had fun without me."

My dad said, "No, baby, you were asleep and I didn't want to wake you. Jewels and I went to the store. We're going to fix your favorite."

"That's so sweet of you two," she said. She called me into her room to remind me of our agreement. I couldn't believe how scared she was of my dad. I knew one day he would find out, but today was not the time. I looked at her and said, "Okay, can we just enjoy this moment." She hugged me and said, "Sure, baby."

Now I'm laying here in my bed, wondering if this is the perfect time to tell him about all the things that have happened to me. I bet my mom was mad about moving to Dallas. I still want to go. I need to get away from all the bad memories in this house. When I first walked into these doors, I thought I was in heaven, but for the last couple of years I've been living in hell.

Adult Life

Tracie

What have I done? Now I know Mike is going to have some questions for me when I get out of this hospital. I just want to die so that I won't have to explain myself. I wonder if Jewels has told him anything about these last couple of years.

Mike and I were high school sweethearts. I remember when we first met. I was walking to the library and he was standing in the student center. He asked me for my phone number. I smiled and told him when I came back from the library that I would give it to him. I smiled all the way there, thinking about him. He had the nicest smile. His teeth were so straight and white. Lord knows how I love a man with pearly white teeth. I walked back to the student center and found him in the same spot waiting for me. I handed him my number and went back to the office. I couldn't believe a junior wanted to talk to me, a freshman. I thought I was doing it for a while especially when he walked me to my classes. He made me feel like he was really feeling me and I loved it.

After Mike graduated from high school, things sort of changed between him and me. He left for college and I had two more years before I would graduate. I suggested we go our separate ways so that he wouldn't be tempted to cheat. Why did I say that? That was the worse choice I could have ever made.

I met a guy, whom turned out to be a thug. I couldn't understand why I was so attracted to him, because he wasn't the kind of guy that I would have wanted to date. Later in the relationship, I

23

found out that he was a pimp. He wanted me to be his main lady. Being the main lady meant that I would make sure all the other girls were happy and well taken care of. I would be responsible for paying them what I thought they deserved. I would also be responsible for taken care of the big spenders that came along.

I told him that being a pimp's main lady was not the lifestyle that I wanted to live. He laughed at me and told me that I was going to be whatever he wanted me to be. Then he grabbed me by the neck until tears started running down my face. He looked into my eyes and said, "Right?" I shook my head up and down, to let him know that I understood how things would be. "Now say, 'Yes, Daddy,'" he said, and I did. After he let my neck go, I began coughing to catch my breath.

That day was the start of an adult life for me. At the age of sixteen, I was having sex with adult men, participating in threesomes with men and other girls that were my age. I could not believe my life had gone so wrong, in only a few months. I continued to be the main lady until I started gaining weight. I thought if I made myself look unattractive that he wouldn't want me anymore. Sure enough, he didn't.

At the age of eighteen, I was released from his stable. I couldn't believe I had actually made it through high school. It was hard to stay focused on my schoolwork, but I knew if I didn't my mom would have become suspicious. After graduation, I left for Grambling State University. I went hoping to find Mike there, but he found me instead.

I was sitting in my dorm room reading a book when I heard a knock at the door. I opened it and there he was looking as fine as he did before he left. I held him so tight and I didn't want to let go. We sat and talked for a while. I didn't have the courage to tell him about my past after we separated.

We started to date again and boy I was glad. He had his way of making me feel so special. We made a vow that we wouldn't separate from each other ever again. One day we were sitting in his car and I asked him if he had ever tried marijuana. He gave me a strange look and said, "No, have you?" I then began to tell him about the many drugs I had tried and he couldn't believe it.

I rolled up a blunt and we began to get high. I closed my eyes and before I knew it, I was taking his clothes off. I don't know what had gotten into me. I started thinking about all the things that I had done and I wanted to do those things with him. I wanted him to experience all the things that I had. There we were, carefree and having wild, crazy sex.

I couldn't keep him off of me after that. We smoked and drank every day. I couldn't believe how happy I was. I asked him if he wanted to do a threesome and he told me no, that's not something he was into. "Whatever we do is just for you and I, that's what makes it so special," he said. My mind was moving like a roller coaster. I thought that was what all men wanted and dreamed about.

Four months later I found out I was pregnant and Mike's attitude changed. He didn't want me to smoke or drink anymore. I was confused. The things that we used to do, he didn't want to do anymore. I tried to stop but it was hard. It seemed as if I couldn't think straight without it. When I smoked, it took me to another level. He kept a close watch on me. I was enjoying all his attention. He made me feel special. I was in love again.

I finally stopped smoking. Lord knows it was hard, but I knew if I didn't I would have lost the man of my dreams. I had a healthy baby girl, nine pounds, and eight ounces, and twenty-one inches long. When she was born Mike was so happy he just stared at her and called her Jewels.

Mike started treating me differently after Jewels was born. All his attention went from me to her. He didn't want me to breast feed because he thought I would start back drinking and smoking. I started to feel like our roles had been reversed.

Jewels and I didn't bond well. I think I started to get a little jealous of all the time that Mike was spending with her. I felt like that time belonged to me. He was supposed to make me feel special, not her. I started to feel lonely inside, and I hated feeling alone. I started working out again so that I could lose some of the baby fat that was left on me while Mike stayed at home with Jewels. I finally got fed up. I built up enough courage to tell him that I thought he was giving Jewels too much time. He couldn't understand how I could say something like that about my own daughter.

One night he got his mother to watch Jewels while he and I went for a ride. He told me how special I was and how much he loved me and asked if I would be his wife.

I couldn't believe what he was saying. With tears in my eyes, I said, "Yes, yes, I would." Mike graduated from Grambling and was on his way back to Los Angeles. He told me that he would take Jewels with him, so that I could finish college. I didn't want to take the chance of losing him, so I left with him.

When we arrived in Los Angeles, we had to stay with his mother for a while. My mother wouldn't dare let us stay with her, she didn't agree with the whole idea of having a baby before marriage. At one point she tried to convince me to have an abortion. I thought about it and decided not to because I knew I would regret it in the future.

Living with his mother was cool at first. She helped a lot with Jewels. Mike went looking for a job while I continued my last few years at UCLA. I could feel a part of me wanting to go back to my old habits, but I knew if I did Mike and I wouldn't last long. Now that I had a baby to think about I didn't want to take the risk.

Two years had passed and living with his mother was working on my nerves. She was acting as if I didn't know what I was doing as a mother. She kept questioning the things that I would do. One day I got so mad that before I knew it, the words, "Shut up, you old hag," came out of my mouth. I knew at that moment it was time for us to look for another place to stay.

I can remember it like it was yesterday. She looked at me and said, "Excuse me, what did you call me?" Why couldn't I just leave it alone? No, I had to repeat myself as if she didn't hear me the first time. The minute I said "hag" again, I felt her right hand come across my face. It took a lot for me not to swing back. She kept saying, "Baby, it's time for you to go."

She went into the room we slept in and started to pack up my clothes. I asked what she was doing, and why did I say that? She looked at me and said, "You stank hoe. Do you think you're going to live in my house after disrespecting me? Jewels can stay, but you got to go."

"I'm not leaving my baby with you," I said.

Mike walked in and his mother started telling him what happened. The look on his face was a look of disappointment and disbelief. He apologized to his mother for weeks. We didn't stay with her much longer after that. Mike found us an apartment up the street. He wanted to stay close to his mother, since she was going to be the one to keep Jewels during the day while I was at school and Mike was at work.

Graduation was a big day for me. That was the first time in a long time that I had seen my aunts and cousins. My mom was so proud of me. She couldn't stop hugging me. Once again, the attention was all on me and I was happy. I don't know why I yearned for so much attention, but I did.

Mike finally got a good job. He wanted us to stay in the apartment for a while until we saved up some money. I didn't have to work since he was making enough to support us. Lord knows I was so happy that I didn't have to go by his mother's house anymore to get Jewels.

I tried my best to bond with Jewels while we were alone together but it seemed as if it just wasn't happening. I love my baby, but for some reason my love wasn't as strong as I thought it should have been.

We ended up staying in the apartment longer than I had expected. Mike lost his job and boy did things turn for the worse. He was depressed all the time and it was making me tired. I got out of the house and started looking for something to do; I needed to hang out with other adults.

I remembered my grandmother telling me that God will supply all your needs if you only believe, so I started talking to God about Mike and asking him to give him strength. I asked God to help us become financially stable so we could move into a house. I was so tired of staying in that small two-bedroom apartment.

I found a job working for a company as a business analyst. They didn't want to pay me what I should have been making because I didn't have any experience. I was okay with that because I knew it would only be temporary. Mike was determined not to put Jewels in daycare, so he stayed home with her. He wanted to wait until she was old enough for school. Jewels grew up fast and before I knew it she was going to elementary. Mike found a job and I was finally planning our wedding.

We were married and I was so excited. Mike's new job started sending him on trips for training classes. He had a feeling they were preparing him for a vice president position. After our wedding, we started to look for a house. I couldn't believe all of these good things were happening at once. My relationship with Jewels started to get better and that made me feel good on the inside. I guess my grandmother was right when she said, "Prayer changes things."

It took some years' worth of training, and Mike was finally promoted to vice president. We were all jumping for joy. I found my dream home in the mountains and I was so glad that we were finally moving out of that apartment. The moment I walked into the house all my prayers were answered, but with the choices I have made these past two years I wonder if the outcome would have been the same if I had kept praying.

I don't understand why I am doing this to my family and myself. I had it made. God gave me all that I had prayed for, and look how I treated it. I guess I wasn't ready for what I thought I wanted. I know I need some help, but I'm not for sure if I'm ready for it.

Confused

Mike

I couldn't sleep last night. I'm really confused and I don't know what to think. Something has been going on and I need to find out what. A brother work his butt off to make sure his family is well taken care of and when he comes back the house is no longer together. I went into Jewels's room to see if I could get more out of her but she was still asleep.

I started looking around to see if I could find something that would help me understand. Something told me to grab one of her books and when I did a letter fell out. I started reading the letter and my heart began to fill up with pain. The woman that I married was not the person that I thought she was.

The hurt began to turn into anger. I began pacing back and forth and crazy thoughts were going through my head. I wanted to kill her. I walked into the kitchen to get a glass of gin and the minute I grab the bottle Jewels walk in. She looked at me with those innocent eyes and asked me if I was going to fix some pancakes and eggs. I put the bottle back and said, "Yes." We sat down at the table and began to talk. I asked her to tell me the truth about what had been going on while I was gone. She stared at her plate in silence. I knew by the reaction to my question that something bad had happened. As she began to tell me about what happened between her and her mom's pimp tears of anger flowed down my face. I could tell that she was reliving the incident all over again.

My mind was full of mixed emotions. I had to keep my composure because I knew if I lost it Jewels would be terrified. I didn't know how to handle this. I failed as the head of the house. As the man of the house you are supposed to always protect your kingdom and I didn't. I started apologizing to Jewels and with tears flowing down her face she said, "It's not your fault." I hugged her so tight I didn't want to let her go. I can't believe her mother sat there and watched a man rape her. I knew I couldn't remain in the same house with her because if I did she would end up dead.

I took Jewels to the doctor to make sure that everything was okay. By the grace of God she was clean. She didn't want me to say anything to the doctors because she knew they would try to do something to Tracie. I couldn't understand after all she had done to her why she would still want to protect her mother. I guess it's true what they say about the bond between a mother and her child.

I dropped Jewels off at my mom's house while I went to the hospital. I knew if I would have told her where I was going she wouldn't have gotten out of the car. I headed toward the hospital full of rage and negative thoughts running through my head. My heart started beating fast the closer I got to the doors of her room.

I walked in and looked her dead in her eyes. She knew something was up. I threw the letter in her lap and asked her to tell me what this was all about. She said that was a long time ago before you and I got married. "How dare you sit there and lie to me in my face?" I said. "So you have a pimp now?" I asked. She didn't say anything. The nurse walked in and asked if everything was okay. I looked at her and said, "Yes." She gave me a funny look and walked out of the door.

Tracie looked at me and said that she didn't want to discuss this at the hospital. I asked her who was the man who raped our daughter and she looked at me and said, "I don't know what you're talking about." At that moment, something inside of me said, "Kill her. Kill her right here right now." I went toward her with my hands going straight to her throat and I heard Jewels's voice saying, "No, Daddy, please don't do it."

30

I turned around and there she was with my mother. I stormed out of the hospital so fast. I heard my mother's voice following me. I didn't pay her any attention. I was ready to attack the first man I saw that looked like a rapist. My mind was out of control going a hundred miles an hour. I never felt my heart ache as much as it does now. My own child has been violated and I couldn't do anything to stop it. I'm going to find this Daddy punk and kill him. I have to prove to my daughter that I am her protector and she can count on me whenever she is in need.

Hospital Room

Jewels

When I walked into the hospital room and saw my dad about to choke my mother my eyes got real big and all I could say was, "No, Daddy." I never saw my dad look that angry before. Why did I tell him about what happened? What have I started? I know my mom is mad at me. Those were the thoughts that went through my head after my dad left. My mom looked at me and said, "Why? Why did you tell your daddy? Now you know whatever happens is your fault. You know Daddy didn't rape you. You wanted it just as much as he did."

"You know he raped me. You saw it with your own two eyes," I said.

She looked at me and said, "Don't act like you're all innocent. You know you were already having sex, oh you didn't think I knew about Troy, did you?" she asked. "In fact, I set the whole thing up. When you started hanging out, I had a private detective follow you around. He gave me the scoop on the guy that you were hanging out with. I got his number and asked him to get to know you a little better. I had to do something to keep you out of my business. I also told him to act like he was falling for you."

I couldn't believe what I was hearing. My own mother set me up to get raped. *Why did she hate me so? Is this how a mother should be?* I thought.

She then began to tell me about how Troy called her up after he was finished with me. She looked at me and said, "'You were all right for a virgin.' Is that what he told you?" and then she started laughing.

I was so angry. My mind went back to that day and all the pain that I was feeling. I started breathing real hard and before I knew it I was choking my mother. I looked in her eyes and watched her try to breath. Her face began to turn red. A tear drop fell down her left eye and then I heard a voice say, "Stop, don't do it." I slowly moved my hands from her throat and said, "No more, no more. I can't take it anymore. I'm tired." I never knew a child could be tired of living at the age of thirteen.

I left out of the room running into my grandmother's arms. She looked at me and asked if everything was okay. I told her yes. My grandmother never knew what happened in that room and if it's up to me she never will.

My mom was in the process of getting released from the hospital when we got there. I wonder how she was getting home since my dad left and I knew my grandmother wasn't going to take her. I had to beg her to bring me up here to see her. I knew I had to get out of her presence so I asked my grandmother to take me home. She took me to a movie because she knew that I was not doing so well. I think that was her way of helping me not to think about things.

After the movie my grandmother dropped me off at the house and boy I knew I was going to walk into a mess. I was kind of scared about what my mom would say to me after choking her. I felt a sense of relief when I got there and nobody was home. I went into my room, locked my door, and went to sleep. I woke up hearing a bunch of loud cussing. I didn't even know anybody was here. From the sound of it I think my dad was just getting home. I looked at the clock and it was 4:00 the next morning. My mom kept lying about the whole rape thing, which hurt me even more. I didn't understand how she could betray her own child. I walked in while they were fussing and stared at my mother. I then asked her why she hated me so. She told me that she never wanted me. If it wasn't for my daddy I would have been dead when she was eight weeks pregnant.

To hear my mother say those words was devastating. I just stood there in disbelief. Then she started telling my dad about Troy and how I let him in the house while she was gone so we could have sex. The look on my dad's face put chills down my spine. I dropped my head and shook it from side to side. I couldn't believe it. She twisted everything around so I would be the one he would be mad at.

My dad looked at my mother and told her that it was over. He told her that he couldn't believe that she was acting like a kid and not holding up to the things that she did wrong. He told me to go pack up my stuff so we could go over to my grandmother's house. My mom started trying to hug him and tell him that she was sorry. She told him that she would get herself cleaned up and that she would change for him. My dad shook his head and said no. He told her that he didn't want her to change for him but for herself. "Your mother didn't raise you to be this way," he said to her. "I know your dad is turning over in his grave. You really need God back into your life," he said. He sent me to my room and they started talking. I never found out what they talked about, all I know is the next day my dad filed for a divorce. She wasn't happy about it at all. She told him that she wanted half of everything that he had. She didn't get it though. He gave her the house and told her that whatever equity she could get would be hers. And that was all he left her with.

Questions

Mike

As I was driving back to the house I thought about all the ladies that I have pushed away because of the love that I had for my wife. All those opportunities that I had but I chose to be faithful and what did being faithful get me, a prostitute. I have to release this anger out fast because if I don't, I don't know what I'm going to do.

Then I remember this lady I met a couple of months ago name Sade. I met her at this conference that my job had sent me on. Her charisma drew my curiosity and I had to get to know her. She made me feel comfortable when she was around and since the doors have been opened for fornication I might as well do it too. Tracie won't be the only one having outside fun.

I called her up and she answered. Her voice took my mind off of what was going on. I asked her if I could come over and she said sure. "There isn't anything wrong with two adults having a little conversation," I said to myself. I drove up to her apartment complex and punched her door number on the gate code pad. She opened the gate and I drove to her apartment. I know you're wondering how I knew where she lived. Well, I've been here before. I almost fell weak to temptation but I turned it down. I got as close as taking her shirt off and then it hit me I had a wife at home. I politely took my hands off her body and walked out of her apartment. That was then and today is a whole new day. I walked into her house and all I could think about was that night I turned away. She asked me if everything was all right and I started telling her my story and tears began to fall slowly down her beautiful face. Sade is light-skinned, about five feet four, weighing at about 130 pounds. She has curves in all the right places and her smell will make a brother weak to his knees. She grabbed me and held me so tight chills went through my body. It was like she was passing something through me with her touch. We caught eye contact and that was it.

We started kissing and she started rubbing me in all the right places and I picked her up and carried her to the room. Her body was so soft. Her curves fit perfectly in my hands. The minute I went inside of her my body melted. The way she moved her body was turning me on more and more. Her moans made my feet curl up. It had been a long time since I had this feeling and I enjoyed every minute of it.

I woke up and it was three o'clock. I knew that I needed to get home to see how Jewels was doing. I wasn't for sure if she had gone home with my mother or not. I kissed her on the forehead and whispered, "I really enjoyed last night and thank you so much for being there for me. I will call you later on today." and then I walked out the door.

I thought about Sade all the way home. I knew she was in my life for a reason and I was ready to find out why. I pulled up in the driveway of the house and my attitude did a 360. I knew I was about to walk in hell and I was ready to fight. I opened the door and there Tracie was sitting on the couch waiting on me. She started asking me questions about where I was and who I been with. I told her she had some nerve to question my whereabouts after all she had done. Then I asked her about the pimp again and she went silent. I asked her to explain to me why she would let a man rape her daughter and watch while it happened. She began to tell me that Jewels lied about the whole rape thing and that she was just trying to break us up. I couldn't believe it. "Of all people, you, the mother, of our child. Why, Tracie?" I asked. "Why would you let something like this happen to her?"

"Why are you taking her side?" she asked.

I shook my head and said, "Sides, you are a grown woman. How are you going to come to me about taking sides? Our daughter told me that she had been raped and I believe her. You have issues that I never knew you had. You really need to get some help. I don't understand how you could do this. I was nothing but a good man to you. I gave you everything you ever wanted and much more. The only thing I didn't give you was a black eye. Is that what you wanted from me?" I asked. "Is that how you think a man shows his love to a woman? I know if you have a pimp he's putting his hands on you. Why in hell do you need a pimp anyway, it's not like you need money?"

"I'm not in love with you anymore, Mike," she said. "I thought you were the one for me but while you were gone I realized that I needed and wanted something more."

"Oh really," I said. "If that is the case, fine, I can understand that, but what did Jewels ever do to you, she's a child?"

"Ever since she's been in this world you have given her all the attention that you were supposed to be giving to me."

"Is this what all this is about?" I asked. "You got to be kidding me. Are you jealous of your own daughter? You carried her for nine months, your bond should be stronger than mine."

She pushed me and said, "You knew I wasn't ready for no baby and I only had her because you wanted me to. And another thing, if you were handling your business in the bedroom I wouldn't have had to go outside."

I smiled at her and said, "Really? Well, that's cool that you feel that way. I know what I have and I know how to work what I have so don't try that high school shit with me. You are supposed to be a grown woman but listening to you talk just lets me know that you are still a child. I was out busting my butt for you."

She screamed out, "No, not for me, for Jewels."

She started telling me how our relationship was just getting close. She started complaining about how she didn't have enough time with me to herself and when Jewels came my focus was not on her anymore but on Jewels.

"What's wrong with you," I asked? "You are a kid in a grown-up's body. Did something happen to you after I left to go to college? You weren't like this when we were together in high school. Is there something that you need to tell me?" She didn't say anything. "This is some bullshit," I said as I started walking out the door.

She screamed, "Wait please don't leave!"

I turned around and told her that she was searching for something that nobody but God could give her. I also told her that I couldn't be with her anymore because if we stayed together, "I wouldn't be able to trust you. And if I can't trust you I won't be faithful to you so why waste my time and yours."

She started to cry and apologize about everything that happened. She told me about how she met Daddy after I left for college and the things that he made her do. She said that he was the one who got her on crack. I looked into her eyes and asked her if he raped Jewels. She dropped her head and said yes. Before I knew it I had knocked her across the room. I started kicking her in her back. Jewels came in and laid across Tracie and said, "No, Daddy, no more."

I couldn't believe what I had done. How could I have let my daughter see me do this to her own mother? This lady pulled something out of me that I didn't know I had. I told Jewels I was sorry and then looked at Tracie as she laid on the floor crying with blood coming down her nose. I shook my head and said, "I'm through. You and this daddy cat are going to jail."

Jewels said, "No, Daddy. I don't want her to go to jail. Please don't call the police. She needs help. Can we get her some help?" Jewels asked.

I said, "I don't think she wants any help."

Jewels turned to Tracie and asked her if she wanted some help. Tracie looked at Jewels and said, "I hate you, get out of my face."

At that moment, I grabbed my things and told Jewels to come on. I could tell by the look on Jewels's face that she was in pain from the words of her mother. When we got into the car and drove off I told Jewels that her mother had a serious problem and she needs help. I told her that I didn't think her mother realized how much help she really needs.

I know Jewels is so confused and counseling will be best for the both of us to do. I can't wait to get to Dallas. Jewels looked out the window all the way to my mom's house. When we got there, she ran into the guest room and closed the door.

My mom asked me what happened and I told her everything. She looked at me and said, "Son, you have to do what's best for your daughter. You probably don't realize it but she's going to be damaged for life if she doesn't get help soon." She talked to me about generational curses that get passed on without anyone getting help. She then said that Tracie's actions seemed like she was a part of a generational curse. I didn't understand it at first until she told me about her mother. She told me that her mother was molested by her stepdaddy and that's how she was conceived. My grandmother had my mother when she was sixteen years old. Her mother didn't believe her and she ended up kicking my grandmother out on the streets. She then told me that when her mom let her come back to stay, her mom's boyfriend had molested her and when she tried to tell her mother she didn't believe her and she ended up getting kicked out the house again.

"This is called a generational curse, and I was determined not to pass that down to my kids. So I moved down here and I got into the word of God and he showed me a different way of living. Son you need to start talking to the lord yourself because you're going to need him to get over all the things that have happened. If you don't then you will hate Tracie for the rest of your life," my mom said.

I knew what she was saying was right. I really hate Tracie right now. I couldn't believe that I put my hands on her and it felt good. My momma taught me better than that. I knew I had to get help and I needed to get it soon. I went to see a counselor by myself first so I could get a better understanding about my feelings.

Dr. Rygalski helped me to express my feelings, and I didn't realize that crying was one way of releasing the built-up anger. She wanted me to talk to Jewels first before I brought her into counseling. She said since Jewels trust me talking to her first about what has happened and going to a counselor would help her feel more comfortable talking to other women. She explained that Tracie's actions toward Jewels would make her look at motherly women different. She said that I should watch out for any new females that I might bring into her life. And to also keep a close eye on Jewels because some of Tracie's traits could have passed on to her.

That scared me. I didn't want my daughter to turn out like her mother. It was like Tracie had built up hate from somewhere and she looked and acted like she was about to break down. I was determined to make sure that Jewels didn't have that problem. I started looking for a place in Dallas. My goal was to be moved by the end of the month.

I asked Sade to help me. She said she used to stay down there and she knew of some nice areas. I had to go down there for a week on business and she took that trip with me. It was something about this woman; her beauty, her glow, and attitude did something to me. I didn't want her to leave my presence. I hope Jewels will accept her.

When we got into our hotel, it was late. We ordered room service, laid down, and watched a movie. It still amazed me how much I enjoyed being with this woman. I felt like we were supposed to be together.

Alone

Tracie

I can't believe that I'm sitting here in this house by myself. What have I done? Are they gone for real? I know he's going to miss me and come back. He won't make it without me and plus we made a vow to stay together forever. I heard a knock on the door and I ran to get it hoping in my heart that it was Mike. When I asked who is it he said "Daddy." My heart dropped. He wasn't the man that I wanted to see. I opened the door and he came in with a look on his face as if he wanted me to do something. I asked him what was up and he told me that he heard through the grapevine that I am living in this big house all by myself. I looked at him and said, "Yes that's true, what is it to you?" He said that he felt it would be a good idea if he ran the stable out of this house. I told him that wouldn't be a good idea because the neighbors here are very nosy and they will call the cops. He told me not to worry about that he knows how to handle the cops. I really wasn't feeling this but what other choice did I have. I messed up so bad that I know if I called Mike, he wouldn't answer. I told him yes. My dream home had turned into a whore house and I couldn't do anything about it.

Daddy kept me drugged up, which helped me maintain my composure with the men he brought my way. My body was starting to get tired. I think I was having sex with about eight different men a day. I couldn't believe that this would be the outcome of my degree.

There were so many people going in and out of my house I didn't know how to keep track. There are four women living here who have their regulars and they come every day like clockwork.

It's been four months and I haven't heard from or even seen Mike and Jewels. I keep thinking about Jewels and the things that I said to her. I can't believe I did that. Was it the drugs that had me act this way? My mind and body looks horrible. My mom keeps calling but I don't answer because I don't know what to say. I always call her back when I know I'm going to get the voicemail so she won't worry about me.

The cops started coming to my house regularly and Daddy didn't know how to handle them like he said he did. He started to get scared and decided to move the stable somewhere else. He also told me that I was getting to old and that no one was requesting my services anymore so he didn't need me.

I couldn't believe what I was hearing. I'm thirty-four years old and nobody wants me. My body is ran over. I weigh about hundred and five pounds and I wasn't looking good at all. I don't have a place to call my own. This house is full of bad memories and I can't stay here anymore.

I got the house put back together and I put it on the market. It sold quickly and I was so glad about that. I ended up getting fifty thousand dollars off the house. I got me a small apartment. I kept ten thousand so I could get me some things for the apartment. I put thirty thousand in a trust fund for Jewels and I set it up so that I wouldn't be able to take any money out. I kept the rest in the bank so I could have when I needed it. I ended up smoking the rest of the money on crack. They kicked me out of the apartment because I got five months behind on my rent. I was out on the streets. I didn't want to go to my mom because I didn't want her to see me like this.

I ended up in a shelter and I met this nice lady name Irene. She reminded me a lot like my grandmother. She took me in and helped me get myself back together. She put me in rehab so I could get cleaned up.

Being in rehab is hard. My first few days here I felt like death was coming around the corner. I've been in here for about three weeks now. My mind has started to clear up which is good because

I'm able to think about a lot of things. I've started having the same dream repeatedly. I didn't understand it at first. I told my counselor about it and she told me to start keeping a journal.

My recovery is going well. I only have another week in rehab. I'm not for sure if I want to leave because I'm scared that I would go back to my old habits. Irene was supporting me all the way and she said that she would stick by me until I'm strong enough. Keeping the journal is helping me a lot. It seems as if someone is trying to tell me something or I must have blocked something that happened to me in my past and it's trying to get out.

The number six keep popping up in my dreams and the words "I hate you" was the way my dreamed ended every night. I was wondering if that was because those were the last words I had said to Jewels. I wanted to know why I was feeling this way. My counselor sent me to see a psychiatrist. She thought that it would be a good idea to get hypnotized. I was scared at first. I was told to never open Pandora's box because you'll never know what you might find in it and whatever is in it could hunt you for the rest of your life.

I asked Irene if she would come with me and she said okay. The rehab center wanted me to go see the psychiatrist before they released me. They wanted to make sure that what I found out wouldn't set me back. I was so nervous when I got there. The lady told me to lie down and to clear my mind. She said, "Tracie, are you ready?"

I said, "I think so. I know this need to be done but I'm scared. I don't know where this will take me. What if there is a good reason why I have blocked a certain part of my life out. Maybe I should leave it where it is."

She looked at me and said, "The only way you can be true to your future is to acknowledge your past. Whatever you went through in your past is the reason for the choices that you have made in your life. The only way you can get delivered is to face your past head on."

I know this is something that I need to do. There is a reason why I have so much hate and thrive for so much attention. I really want to have a relationship with my daughter and if I don't get myself together, it will never happen. "Okay, I'm ready," I said.

"Okay, close your eyes. I'm going to count to ten. Breathe in and out slowly, one, two, three, four, five, six, seven, eight, nine, and ten. Tracie, I want you to think back. You're six. Do you remember?"

"Yes," I said.

"So what do you see?" she asked.

"I'm playing with my mom. We're having a tea party. I was so happy. We had our hats and gloves on. She keeps telling me that she can't play long because my stepdad would be here soon. I couldn't understand why my mom couldn't spend any time with me when he was around."

"What's happening now?" she asked.

"My stepdad is calling my mother's name. She told me that she would be right back. I'm waiting at the table with my teacup, I'm starting to cry, and I began to call out her name. Momma, momma, come here. I'm walking out of my room looking for her and I don't see her. I opened up the door in her room and I see my stepdad in the bed. I asked him where my mom was and he said she was gone. He's telling me to come here. I got in the bed with him. He's trying to put me up under the covers but I don't want to do it. He keeps telling me how cute I look in my tea dress. He told me to sniff this white candy in my nose. I'm sniffing it and he's laughing. I'm coughing and it seems as if I'm getting dizzy because my head is falling back. He starts to kiss on me and I'm not fighting. Why am I not fighting? He's raping me. Why am I not moving? My mom walks in and she's screaming something. He jumps up and she's going to the dresser drawer. She got a gun and shot my stepdaddy. I'm still lying on the bed. My mom is picking me up. She's crying."

"Take a deep breath." I can hear the psychiatrist say, "Breathe in, now breathe out, let's bring you back to the present. When I finish counting, you will come to and remember everything," she said.

She begins to count: ten, nine, eight, seven, six, five, four, three, two, and one. I opened my eyes and she asked me how I felt.

"Kind of tired and drained," I said. She told me that was normal because my mind was doing a lot of work. She asked me what I thought about the memories and I didn't know what to think. All my life I thought my stepdad died because of a disease he had and now I find out that my mom killed him. I can't believe that I was raped at the age of six. I started thinking about Jewels and how she must have felt. Tears began to flow down my face. I felt like I didn't deserve to live.

The psychiatrist explained to me that what happened to me in the past was the reason for my behavior that I had all these years. I told her about my pimp and she said that he triggered all those feelings. He took your mind back to your past without you even realizing it.

I couldn't stomach what I had just found out. The psychiatrist wanted me to continue to come every week for a while. Due to the program, she was able to provide me services at no charge. I was released out of rehab into Irene's care. She allowed me to stay with her so I wouldn't have to live in the shelter.

Irene talked to me about God and how he loves all. She told me if I was going to stay with her I had to go to church. I was a little uncomfortable at first because I really didn't believe that I deserved to go. She took me to their substance abuse ministry. I couldn't believe how many people had experienced the same thing that I gone through.

Going to church helped me build up my strength and I was starting to feel real good about myself. I stayed with Irene for about six months. I couldn't believe I missed my daughter's fourteenth birthday. It had been a year and a half since I had seen her last. Mike was right. What I was searching for no man could give it to me, only God.

I am so proud of myself. I have been clean for almost a year now. I joined the church and the substance abuse ministry. My life is looking up. Irene got me a job where she works as a file clerk. I was so happy to be making it on my own. For most of my life a man was taking care of me and now that I have God in my life he's showing me that if I trust in him he will supply all of my needs.

I want to write Jewels a letter but I'm not sure on how to begin. I need to make things right between us. I don't want her to be scarred because of me. It was hard at first but once I got through the first two sentences the words started to flow.

Dear Jewels,

It's been a long time since I've seen and spoke to you. I don't blame you if you never want to see me or speak to me again. I've been getting the help that I needed to put my life back together. It has been hard. I'm sorry that I missed your birthday. After you and your daddy left my life went downhill. I started doing the drugs bad. I ended up selling the house and going to a shelter. I met this lady named Irene who helped me get my life back together. I'm going to church now and I've been clean for over a year. I've joined the substance abuse ministry so that I can continue to get the support I need and so I can also help someone else who might be going through the same thing. I miss you so much and I'm sorry for all the things that I have done to you and that I have allowed to happen to you. What I did was wrong and you didn't deserve to be treated like that. I didn't realize it until I went to see a psychiatrist that I was battling with some issues that happened to me when I was a child. I really want to come see you and hope that we can become friends. I know that you probably hate me and who can blame you. With the money that I got from the house, I put you up a trust fund. I know your daddy probably already have one for you. Please forgive me, I'm begging you. I didn't realize how much I would miss you until you left. I was too busy trying to get attention instead of giving you the attention. Here is the number and address where I'm staying. Please call me at 310-555-5555 or write me back if you feel like it. The address is on the envelope.

Love always
Tracie....

I sent the letter to his mother's house hoping that she would send it to her. All I can do now is continue to get myself together so I can be ready if she decides to call.

It's been three months and I haven't heard from Jewels. I don't know how to feel because I really don't know if she received the letter. Maybe she got it and she just doesn't want to talk. Who can blame her? I can't let this discourage me though.

Irene helped me get a place in her apartment complex. She wanted to keep me close by. I had my own place and I was scared. I had never been by myself before and the last time that I was alone, I ended up back with Daddy. I didn't want to go that route. Irene encouraged me more and more and I was so glad that God sent her my way.

We went shopping for furniture and that was fun. After I got my apartment together I told Irene that I wanted to talk to my mom about what had happened to me and I was wondering if she didn't mind being here with me for support. She was happy to help me.

I called my mom up and boy was she mad. She was screaming and yelling, telling me how worried she'd been and was wondering why I haven't called her. I started telling her about what I had gone through. It was pure silence on the phone. I didn't know what had happened. I kept saying "hello" and then she finally said, "I'm here." I could tell she had been crying.

She started telling me how she thought I wouldn't remember since I was so young when it happened. She was so upset with herself because she didn't see the signs. She told me that I had told her that he had been doing this for a couple of months. I told her that I was doing a whole lot better and that I was in church. She wanted me to come by so she could see me and hold me. She said that she had been praying for me and that God kept her at peace. I told her that I would come by next weekend. I was working during the week and had different meetings that I had to go to after work.

She kept telling me how much she loved me and that she was sorry for what I had to go through. I told her I didn't blame her for what happened and that I'm just glad that she kept praying for me. I hung up the phone with my mother and Irene gave me a big hug and told me how proud she was of me.

I asked her what made her be a volunteer at the shelter. She started telling me about how her mother chose her boyfriend over her and because of the lack of attention she began hanging out and having sex at an early age. She ended up getting pregnant and at the age of sixteen, her mother kicked her out of the house. She was telling me how scary it was being out there all alone.

Her friend's parents wouldn't let her stay with them because they felt she was a bad influence. She then told me that she ending up getting an abortion because the boy who got her pregnant didn't want the baby. Her story sounded a little bit like mine. I started thanking God after I heard her story because I knew that this was all in his plan and that he never gave up on me. I went to bed for the first time in peace knowing that no matter what happens from this day forth God has my back as long as I continue to put him first.

Dallas

Mike

We've finally made it to Dallas. I hope Jewels like the house Sade and I picked out. It's not as big as the house before but it's enough for the two of us. I'm still in shock over the whole thing with Tracie. I really loved her. I thought she was the one that I was going to grow old with but I guess you never know how things are going to end up. It was hard leaving but I know it was the best thing for Jewels. I hope that things will get better for Tracie but I can't worry about her. I have our child to think about.

Sade said that she would love to move back to Dallas if I wanted her to. I didn't know what to say. I don't want her to move because of me. I like her a lot but I don't want her to change her life just for me. I'm not for sure if she and Jewels will get along. I want to introduce her to Jewels but I'm not sure if Jewels is ready. Jewels took the incident with her mother very hard. She stayed in her room for weeks. I didn't know what I was going to do. It took her a while but she finally came out of her room. She came out with questions. She wanted to know why her mother would hate her so and if she would ever find it in her heart to love her. All I could say is all things are possible with prayer.

I don't think she really understands how a mother is supposed to be to a daughter so however Tracie treated her is how she think it should be. I hope that she will be able to see how a real mother is supposed to be to her child. The choices we make can bind us for the rest of our lives. Why did I knock on Tracie's door that day, if I had only stayed away?

Oh well, that's not how my life turned out so I have to play the cards that has been dealt and make the best of the life that I have. School is starting soon and I hope Jewels find her a friend. Having a friend can help you get through things in life. I found a therapist that specializes in family crisis for youth, and I'm just waiting on the perfect time to schedule the appointment.

I'm trying to focus on the new job and it's not easy. When things are not going well at home it is hard to concentrate on anything else. I wonder what Sade is doing. I wish she was here now. I know she would have something good to say to make me feel better.

I never realized how lonely it was being without someone in your life. Even though I was gone a lot I always knew that I had a wife at home to go to. Now I'm laying here in my bed wondering what I'm going to do. My daughter is traumatized and this is something that I never had to face. You can throw a business question at me and I will know how to tackle it from A to Z, but my own child; I really don't know where to start. Jewels ran into my room crying about how she misses her mother and how she wonders if she's doing okay. I really thought Tracie would have contacted her by now. I couldn't do anything but hug her and tell her that everything would be all right. Those words came out my mouth but I really had my doubts. She laid in my arms and cried herself to sleep. I looked up at the ceiling with my mind full of random thoughts wondering whether or not I will be able to handle this all by myself.

The next morning Jewels woke up with a different attitude. She was in the kitchen making pancakes. I grabbed the bowl and begin mixing up the eggs. This reminded me of the old days. She was acting like nothing ever happened. I didn't know how to take this. I just went along with it. After breakfast we went for a ride around the neighborhood. I was hoping that she would see some kids outside that she would want to meet.

She started telling me how she was ready for the summer to be over with so she could go to school. She was tired of being in the house. She said she needed something to do so she wouldn't have to think about what happened. I understood what she was saying. I used the job to keep my mind occupied and she doesn't have anything.

I asked her if she wanted to go shopping and she said she wasn't feeling it right now. I drove back home. She went into the living room and started watching TV. I needed to talk to somebody and my mother was the first person that came to mind.

I called my mom and told her how things were going and she told me that it was going to be hard at first but not to give up. She said that Tracie sold the house and she moved into an apartment. She also said that after we left Tracie got on that stuff real bad and started running a whore house out of the house. I didn't want to believe what I was hearing but I knew that drugs could make a person do some crazy things. She wasn't for sure what she was doing now. She hadn't heard any new news. In my heart I was hoping that she turned out all right. I know how much Jewels wants a relationship with Tracie. I hope she doesn't wait too long. Once Jewels get to a certain age she's not going to care. I thought my mom was going to ease my mind but she only put more on it.

The phone rings and its Sade.

"Hey, how are you doing?" she says.

"I'm fine, just thinking about Jewels. She seem like she was coming around today but I don't know if it's an act."

"Well, Mike, just keep a close watch on her. She's probably trying to come around slowly."

"You're probably right. I just hate to see my baby like this."

"I know. Hey, I'm still thinking about moving down. There is room for me at the facility in Dallas."

"Are you sure you want to do this? I mean, I don't want you to make this big change for me."

"I can say you're my motivation. I came to LA to get away from my folks down there but now I found a reason to come back."

"I really would love your help. I know Jewels need a positive woman in her life. I don't want her to grow up thinking that's how a mother is supposed to be."

"Mike, I can't take the place of her mother. I can only be a friend. I can try to help her in ways by showing her how a lady is supposed to be and communicate with her about how a parent should be."

"Anything is better than nothing. I'm trying to find a good time to introduce you to her. I don't want to move too fast and then she turns against you."

"She's not going to accept me too well at first but that's to be expected. Just let me know when you're ready. I'm coming down in a couple of months to see my mother. I will let you know when I arrive. While I'm there I will be looking for a place. Keep your head up, Mike. You are a strong black man and I know that you can do it."

"I hope you're right, Sade. Thanks for being a friend."

"No worries, that's what friends are for."

We hung up the phone and I laid down and closed my eyes. In my heart I really want things to go well between Jewels and Sade. Why didn't I meet her before all of this happened. I can't dwell on that. How will I know when the right time will be? I guess only time will tell.

Two months have passed and school is starting in a couple of days. I haven't seen Jewels this excited about school in a long time. We went shopping for school clothes and boy did I see the old Jewels come back to life. She went into every store in the mall it seemed.

Violated

Jewels

My dad found us a nice house in Dallas. It wasn't as big as the house in LA but I was okay with that. I still had my own room and my own bathroom. I was cool. I can't believe my own mother treated me like that.

My dad and I had to go to counseling for a while. He couldn't get over the guilt that he was carrying for the things that had happened to me. He watched my every move and anyone who came close to me he was right there. He really took the protection thing out of control, but who can blame him. I enjoyed seeing my dad every day. The love and attention he was giving me was what I was missing all this time.

I don't know how to react to all of this. Going to counseling was cool but I still feel empty inside. I really want a relationship with my mother but I don't think I will ever get it. I haven't heard or seen her in over a year. She wasn't there when we left the house for good so I didn't have a chance to say good-bye. I wonder how she is doing. I know the drugs had her acting the way she did. Even though she did those things to me, I still miss her.

She missed my fourteen birthday. I thought she would at least call or something. I guess those words she said to me were true. How can a mother have so much hate for her own daughter?

As I sit here in my room I'm wondering if I should commit suicide. Why should I continue to live a life of pain? I continue to have these bad dreams about my past. I can't seem to get the pictures out of my head. I hate myself, when I look into the mirror I see an ugly girl with no hope of happiness. Why would anyone want to be with someone who's been misused and abused? I miss my friends in LA. I thought moving here would be a good thing but it's a little boring without someone to talk to.

I grabbed a knife out of the kitchen and went into my bathroom. I sat down on the floor and begin to rub the knife against my arm. My hands begin to shake with fear and tears started falling down my face. As I pressed down harder against my skin my mind started hearing voices. I can hear them say, "Angel, it's not your time, I'm not finished with you yet." I got up and looked out the door and no one was there. I locked the bathroom door back and sat back down on the floor. As I began to press the knife against my skin I heard the voice again saying, "Angel, it's not your time, I'm not finished with you yet." I dropped the knife on the floor and laid down crying asking God, "Why, why is it not my time? I been through enough and I can't take it anymore."

Before I knew it, I began saying, "Help me, Lord, I need you now. Please, Lord, help me. My soul feels weak and my hope and desire to live is almost gone." I closed my eyes and before I knew it my dad started knocking on the door. "Angel, are you okay in there?" he asked. You've been in there for a couple of hours now. I got up and hid the knife underneath the sink. "Yes, I'm fine." I told him that I'll be out in a minute. I started to wash my face and when I looked in the mirror I saw this glow about me. I couldn't understand it. My mind didn't feel so heavy and I had a burst of energy. I opened the door and there my daddy was looking at me with this funny expression on his face.

"What's going on?" he asked.

"Nothing, I just had a lot on my mind and I needed to be in a quiet space."

"Is it something that you want to talk about?"

"Not right now. I'm still trying to understand it myself."

"You're not pregnant, are you?"

"No, Daddy. You don't have to worry about that."

"Okay, when you are ready to talk I'm here. You are my angel and I love you so much. I don't know what I would do if something were to happen to you."

He grabs me and holds me tight. I really needed a hug at that moment. I don't know what I was thinking about, that would have hurt him so if I had killed myself. I can't do that to him. I love him too much for that.

I walked into my room and turned on the TV. I started flipping the channels and stopped to listen to this speaker. She started talking about how the devil will make you feel like you don't deserve to live and how he will rewind your past over and over again to make you feel like you are not worthy. She began telling the story of the time she was thirteen and her mother's boyfriend molested her. She told her mother and her mother didn't believe her. She said that her mother kicked her out of the house. Here she was at the age of thirteen with nowhere to live. She tried going to her aunt's house but she didn't want to have anything to do with her. Then she said she met this girl who introduced her to the strip clubs. At the age of thirteen she was working the poles. I couldn't believe it. Someone has been where I've been and to think I thought I was the only one.

Then she spoke of how she was getting tired of dancing in front of those old men so one day she sat in her apartment and began taking pills. Every pill she found she took. She fell on the ground and she said she saw her life flash before her eyes. She then began to feel happy and free. She saw a new life, a new beginning. When she opened her eyes all she saw were nurses staring at her. At that moment tears fell down her face. Her friend had found her on the floor and called the ambulance. Her friend looked at her and said, "Girl, I guess it wasn't your time and God has some angels out there watching over you because the doctor said I found you just in time."

She turned and looked straight at the camera as if she was looking directly at me and said, "If you are out there and you're feeling like life has gotten you and you can't take it anymore and you feel suicide is the way to go, please understand that killing yourself is not the answer. You must know that God has a plan for your life and all you have to do is trust in Him and believe." All the words she spoke hit home. It was as if she knew what I had just tried to do. I can't believe that no matter how much mess I went through God can still have a plan for my life.

After that I started looking at life differently. I really believe in my heart that God has a purpose for my life and that He is going to use me to help someone else.

School is in and there is this boy at school that likes me. I'm scared to talk to him because I don't know how to tell if they're being true to the relationship. I found me a new friend at school. She's a little different. I think she likes girls. This is something that was new to me. I didn't think girls were supposed to date other girls.

We started hanging out and she told me how she started to be with girls. She told me that when she was young the next-door neighbor's daughter used to mess with her. At first, it was confusing to her and then it lasted so long that she thought this was how things were supposed to be. Until one day she tried it on a friend from school and she told her that wasn't normal.

She told me that she stopped for a while and tried dating boys but they didn't please her like the neighbor's daughter did. My mind was confused. At the age of fourteen this girl thinks she should be dating other girls. I knew in my heart that wasn't right but I wasn't going to judge her, and besides I've been through so much in my life up until now I don't have room to judge anyone.

After I told her what happened to me she tried convincing me that it only made sense for me to date girls, since the guys have been treating me so bad. What she said sounded good, but something inside of me kept saying that it wasn't right. I told her that I didn't roll like that. I also told her that I would still be her friend as long as she doesn't try anything with me.

She was cool about it. The kids at school started calling me names because I hung with her but I didn't care. I was surprised that it didn't hurt me any. I guess I had gone through so much, that their words didn't carry much weight. Natalie's girlfriend started getting jealous of our friendship and broke it off with her. She cried in my arms for a long time.

I thought, *It doesn't matter if it's a girl or a boy the pain is still the same.* Then she tried it. I guess she thought I was so deep in her pain that she would try kissing me. I jumped back and said, "Natalie, I told you that I didn't go that way. Do you want to have two broken relationships?" She started apologizing and telling me that she wouldn't dare do that again. I told her that we would have to chill from hanging out for a while. I didn't want to have to kick her butt because she was on some kind of emotional trip. Then she started saying how she wouldn't have anyone if I stopped being her friend.

I started feeling sad for her and said okay. I told her if she tried that again I would have to hurt her. After that night, I began to pray for my friend Natalie. I knew that she was confused and only God could pick her up and heal her.

Those words reminded me of my granny. It's been a long time since I've seen her. I told my daddy that I wanted to go spend a week with her during the summer. He made the arrangements and I marked my calendar. I asked Natalie if she wanted to go and she said okay. My dad even paid for her trip. Natalie's mom lives in the projects and they don't have much money. I think that was one of the reasons why she didn't have that many friends. She always acted as if she was so tough. Yep, you guessed it, she was the guy in the relationship, but was acting like a little girl when her girlfriend broke up with her.

Her mom reminded me of my mom. Living life fast and doing drugs. She told me that her mom was a stripper and every night she had to go over her neighbor's house so she didn't have to stay at home by herself. One day the neighbor's daughter wanted to play a game with her and that's when the molestation began. "It felt weird and I didn't think it was right but since she was the oldest I felt like it was, I mean she should know better than me," Natalie said. As time kept passing Natalie started getting tired of her just doing whatever she wanted to do to her. She said she was so happy when she was old enough to stay by herself because she was getting real tired of the neighbor's daughter messing with her. It was because of her that she felt like she was supposed to be with girls.

One day I went over to her house to play and her mom kept telling me how smart and cute I was. I could tell by the look on Natalie's face she was upsetting her. I asked her about it and she said that her mother never told her those things. She's always saying how much I look like a boy and that she bet I would end up liking girls.

I couldn't believe it. Her mom was doing the same thing to her that my mom was doing to me but using different words. At that moment, I knew what she was going through. I knew why she was so confused with her sexuality.

I told my dad about her. I asked him if we could take her shopping and he said, "Yes." My dad told me how proud he was of me. I didn't tell him that she liked girls because I didn't know if he would take that too well. I told Natalie that we were going to play dress up. She didn't know we were getting the clothes for her.

She would go pick up clothes and then put it down because of the price. I told her not to look at the price and to pick what she wanted. She had so much fun. We ended up spending over a thousand dollars. Her eyes got real big when she saw the total amount on the cash register. She looked at me and said you have that much money. I told her, "I didn't but my dad did."

I took her to a spa. She was so surprised. At first she didn't want to do it. She didn't feel all that comfortable with taking her clothes off in front of strangers. I told her that she would take her clothes off and wrap a towel over her body. She then asked me to stay in the room with her while the person did it. She insists that a man rub her instead of a lady. If I didn't know what she had been through, I would have thought that was kind of weird. I would always ask for a lady.

As she began taking her clothes off I noticed some bruises on her back. I asked her about them and she didn't want to talk about it. I knew something wasn't right. I left it alone because I didn't want to ruin her moment. When he was finished, she went into the other room and got her feet and nails done. I could tell by the look on her face that she was enjoying herself. I never thought seeing someone else happy would make me feel good on the inside.

Then it happened, the hair. She fought me hard on this one. I don't know why she thought that one ponytail was going to work forever. She kept saying how she was cool with everything else and that she didn't want anyone to touch her hair. I asked her if she trusted me, and she said, "Yes." I told her that I wouldn't let anyone do anything bad to her. I could tell by the look on her face that she was scared. When the lady took her ponytail down her hair fell down her back. I didn't know this girl had so much hair. It was so thick and long. All this time I thought her hair was short. The lady looked at her and said, "My, you're such a beautiful young lady and you have such beautiful hair."

Natalie began to smile and from that day forward that smile stayed on her face. Natalie loved how the lady did her hair. She evened it out and put some twists in the front. I told my daddy that I would use my allowance money to get her hair done when I go. My dad said God is going to bless me for thinking of others, but not to get caught up in helping because I can end up getting used. I told him that God wouldn't allow that. He then said, "Yeah you're right, but sometimes we can be so caught up that we don't listen to the words of God. Just make sure that you're helping her and not hindering her." I was a little confused. I didn't know that doing for people could be a hindrance to them. I kept those words in the back of my mind. I knew one day I would understand what he meant by that.

The guys at school loved the new Natalie and she loved the attention. One day she sat down and told me she wanted to try boys again. I asked her what she meant by that and she said she wanted to go with a boy so she can really see if she could have a relationship with one. I told her to go for it. I also told her to be careful because I didn't want her to grab the wrong guy and he mess her up so bad that she will never speak to another guy in that way again.

She met this guy name Brent. He was real cool and suave. He asked her out on a date and I asked her if she was ready. She said she thought so but wanted to know if I could go. I told her that my daddy wouldn't let me go out on a date. I said that I could see if he would let us hang out at my place and watch movies. She said, "Cool."

I really didn't want to go to my dad and ask him if boys could come over. I knew that he would have trouble with it because of what happened to me in the past. I walked into his room and asked him if it would be okay for Natalie to spend the night. He said, "Cool." Then I asked him if we could have a date over. He looked at me and said, "What kind of date?" Then I told him that there is a boy at the school that I liked, and I wanted to know if he and a friend could come over and watch a movie. He paused and looked at me for a moment. Then he said, "Yes." I couldn't believe it. He said that he would invite a friend to. I thought too, *I know my daddy is not trying to be in the same room with us.* I said, "Okay," and walked out.

I told Natalie that everything was cool for Friday. I also told her that my dad said she could spend the night. We were so happy. I asked Natalie what her mom thought about the new clothes and she said she was cool. The way she said it made me think something wasn't right. I left it alone. I knew one day she would open up to me.

I haven't had a boyfriend since Troy. I'm not sure if I'm ready to make this step but I know Natalie need some proof that all boys are not dogs. I'm going to find the courage and go through with it. I will be sixteen soon and it's time for me to start doing high school kid stuff. I wonder who Brent is going to bring with him. The day I decide to do this dating thing again it ends up being a blind date. I hope this guy isn't ugly. Oh well it's all for fun.

As I was getting ready for bed the phone rang. I wonder who this could be calling this time of night. It was Brent. He caught me off guard at first and then we started talking. I asked him if he had talked to Natalie and he said that he didn't want her, he wanted me. I told him that Natalie was looking forward to seeing him this weekend and asked him who he was going to bring. He said his friend was him, I was like hold up. I clicked over and called Natalie and told her to listen to this mess Brent was talking. I clicked back over and I said, "What do you mean you are the friend."

He started telling me how he liked me the moment that I walked in the school building. He also said that he was using Natalie to get closer to me. I started feeling bad because she had to hear all this. But I didn't think she would have believed me if she didn't. I told him that I had to pass because Natalie is my best friend and I don't do my friends like that. He couldn't believe that I turned him down. He was cute and on the football team but he's not worth losing a friend, especially one that is crying out for help. I hung up the phone and called Natalie back.

She was mad at him. I told her to let it go. He wasn't all that anyway. Knowing good and well that boy had it going on. I asked her if she still wanted to hang out this weekend and she said sure. She also said that she wasn't for sure if her mother was going to let her go out of town with me. She finally told me that her mother wasn't all that happy with the clothes, and she was making her give them back to me. I asked her, "Why?" She said that it wasn't fair to her other sister and brother. If they couldn't have nice things then she couldn't either. I told her she could leave them over my house and change clothes before and after school. She was happy to hear that. She had gained so much confidence in herself since the makeover. I didn't want that to go away. I told my dad the date was off but Natalie still wanted to stay. He said cool and that his friend was still coming because he wants me to meet her. I said okay and went to my room.

I was a little worried at first. It's been the two of us for some time now and now someone else might be added to the picture. I'm not sure if I'm ready to share my daddy with someone else. I wonder if that was how my mom was feeling about me. I guess I will just wait and see how things turn out.

It was two o'clock Friday morning and there was a knock on my window. I got up and looked through it and it was Natalie. She was crying and she was covered in blood. I opened up the window and pulled her in. I asked her what happen she said that her mother had kicked her out because she walked in on her and her ex-girlfriend.

I was like, "What! I thought you had stopped?" She said that her ex came over to talk and then she started kissing on her and before she knew it one thing led to another and then her mother walked in on them. I told her to go into the bathroom and get cleaned up. I got on my knees and asked the Lord to guide me through this. I knew that it had to be an evil spirit that didn't want to let her go.

My grandmother taught me a lot about spiritual warfare and this was one. When she came out of the bathroom she couldn't stop crying. She said when her mom walked in she started beating her in the head and face saying that she didn't raise no dike. She kicked her ex out and told her if she ever sees her around Natalie again she would kill her.

I couldn't believe what I was hearing. First she looked at me and started calling me out of my name. Then she punched me in my face and my nose started bleeding. I ran out the house so fast all I could hear her say was, "Don't come back until you figure out that you are a girl and not a boy." Natalie looked at me and said, "What am I going to do, I don't have a place to stay?"

I told her that God would make a way. "It's time for you to make a decision," I said. "Are you going to trust in God and allow him to really clean you up or are you going to continue to let the devil play with you?"

She said that she was ready to make that change in her life.

We got down on our knees and she began to talk to the Lord. I was shocked because I didn't think she knew him at all. I always thought that people who are out in the world didn't know God or just didn't believe in Him. I guess I was wrong. I could feel the spirit come into my room. She started shouting, "Thank you, Jesus," and in my mind I was like, "Lord, please don't let her wake up my daddy."

I made her a pallet on the floor and we went to sleep. The next morning, when we woke up, I could tell she was still feeling bad about last night. I tried my best to cheer her up but it didn't work.

We got to school and her ex came to her and started apologizing. Natalie told her that it would be best if she didn't speak to her for a while. She also told her that she had decided to bring that part of her life to an end. Her ex started talking loud asking her if I was her new girlfriend. I gave her this crazy look and said that I don't roll like that. She looked at me and said that's what they all say. I wonder if everyone thought I was gay because I hung out with Natalie. I hope not. If they did, oh well, I'm not here to please anyone.

After school, Natalie came over to the house and we talked about how she was feeling. She was a little confused because she didn't know what was going to happen. She wasn't for sure if her mother was serious about her not coming back to the house.

I talked to my dad about it and he was not real sure how to handle it. He really didn't want to get involved. I asked him if he would talk to her mother, he thought about it for a minute and asked me what I was trying to get out of this. I told him that I didn't want to see my friend out in the street.

I know she has a good heart and she has been trying to change for the better. I would hate to see her go back to her old ways just because no one stopped and paid attention to her cry for help. I told him that I watched my mother cry for help for months and I didn't do anything because I didn't think I could, and now that I know someone who is crying out for help I would like to help them.

My dad looked at me and said, "Okay, however, if I get cursed out you owe me dinner." I told him that I would have some money saved. Then he said, "You would have to cook it."

I said, "What, Daddy, you know I don't know how to cook."

He said, "Well, you better call your granny and find out."

"That's not fair," I told him.

He just walked out the room.

"Are you still having company?" I yelled as he was walking down the hallway.

He said, "Yes."

Natalie and I started thinking about things we could do this weekend. I wanted to get her mind off her troubles until my dad spoke with her mother. "How about the movies?" I asked. "My grandmother would always take me to the movies when I was going through some things."

She said, "Cool."

It's Friday night and I can't wait to see this friend of my daddy. I wonder if I'm going to like her. I hope she doesn't try to be all hip or even try to be my friend. Why does he have to have a friend anyway? I think we are doing fine by ourselves.

I have three more weeks until I leave to spend a week with my grandmother and I can't wait. I hope Natalie is still able to come. She's starting to feel a little bit better. I'm so surprised that her mother hasn't called to make sure that she's okay. I know she has to be bothered by that. It's bothering me and she's not my mother.

I haven't spoken to my mother in a long time and I wonder if she even thinks about me. I know she probably doesn't especially after she expressed to me how much she hated me. I really thought after we left she would realize how much I meant to her. I guess that's not true. Oh well I can't worry about me right now, my friend Natalie needs me and plus my mind has to be clear so I can be able to read this new friend of my daddy.

The doorbell rang and my heart began to beat fast. I don't know why I'm so nervous but I am. She walks in and I must admit my daddy has good taste. She looks so sweet and innocent. I've heard about those types at school. Natalie and I walk downstairs from my bedroom and my dad introduces her to us. "Her name is Sade," he says. She shakes our hands and sits down on the couch. Then she asks, "How is Dallas?"

"It's cool."

"And school?"

"School is cool too, so are you and my daddy serious?"

"We're just friends at the moment."

"Oh, at the moment, so something might happen in the near future."

"Your dad and I haven't discussed that yet."

Dad jumps in and asks Sade if she wants something to drink. She says, "Yea." He then tells me to go and get her a cup of water. Natalie and I walk into the kitchen. I asked Natalie what she thought of her and she said that she was all right.

"Yea, but I know something is up with her. I just can't figure it out."

"You just met her. How can you tell something is up?"

"I just know."

We walked back in the living room and I gave her the cup. She said, "Thank you," and then I begin asking her more questions.

"Do you live here?"

"No, I live in LA"

"So you met my dad in LA?"

"Yes on a business trip."

"What kind of work do you do?"

"I'm a CEO for a marketing department. As a matter of fact, they're moving me here."

She looks at my dad and says, "That's the surprise I had to tell you."

My dad smiled and said, "Oh really."

I started playing the detective again knowing in my mind that I'm going to find something that's not right about her. Dinner was good. We had smothered chicken, rice, corn on the cob, and cornbread. I am so full. I must give it to her. The lady knows how to cook. The way her and my dad was working together in the kitchen reminded me of how he and my mother used to be.

I told Sade that it was nice to have met her, and Natalie and I went upstairs.

"I hope she doesn't think she's going to come in this house to be a mother to me."

"If she did, that wouldn't be a bad thing," Natalie said.

"I heard that stepmothers are no good and I really don't want to experience that."

"I don't think every stepmother is bad. You just have to pray that your father finds the right person to be with. I don't think my mother thinks about those things when she brings a man into the house. As long as he can pay the bills he can come in. It seems as if your daddy is a real smart man and he looks after you. I think he will make sure that he brings nothing but the best for you."

"That's true. It has been a long time since he's had anyone in his life. What if I start to like her? I'm scared that I would like her more than I would like my mother."

"I don't think you should worry about that. Your mother is going to always be your mother and no one else can take that away from you. It's okay to love people. Don't look at it as taking your mother's place but as someone who is trying to help."

"You surprise me. All this time and I didn't think you had that in you. You're right. I'm going to think positive until something happens."

"Jewels, you have helped me a lot and I want to thank you. Not too many people have come my way to help the way you have. Everyone that has come into my life has used me and that's how I thought everybody was. You helped me see things differently."

"I guess God has placed us together for a reason. Girl, I can't wait until we go to see my grandmother. You're going to love her. She is the sweetest lady you can ever meet."

"I don't know if my mom is going to let me go."

"Well she kicked you out so I guess it doesn't matter to her. My dad is going to talk to her."

"I don't know if he should. My mother is crazy. She probably will cuss him out."

"That's what he said. I hope she doesn't because if she does I will have to cook him something to eat. Girl, I don't know how to cook."

"Maybe Sade can teach you. Her chicken was really good."

"I don't know. I will wait until I get to my grandmother's house. I don't want to move too fast with her."

"Jewels, just remember you can't judge her. Keep an open mind because you don't know why God has placed her in your path. Girl, I'm starting to sound like you."

"I know. It's amazing to see how much you have changed since the first time we met."

"I know my life wasn't going right, I just didn't know how to change it."

"Jewels," I hear my dad say, "come downstairs."

"I know he wants to ask me questions about Sade. I will be right back," I said to Natalie as I walk out of my bedroom door. I walked into his room and sure enough, he asks me what I think.

"She was cool, Dad, and I think you have nice taste."

He smiles and says, "Oh really, you know she will be coming over more once she has moved here."

"Do you like her more than my mom?"

"Your mother will always have a special place in my heart. The love I have for her is different from how I feel for Sade. I really like Sade. I haven't spent enough time with her to be in love with her."

"I see. I'm glad that you have found a friend, Dad."

He smiled and said, "Me too," as I walked back upstairs to my room.

By the sound of my father's voice and the look on his face, I think he really likes her. I wonder if he's ready for another relationship. I know I'm not ready for him to have one.

Never Give Up

Mike

I'm so glad that the meeting with Jewels and Sade went well. That was something that I was really worried about. Now I have to call this lady and talk to her about her child. I don't know how I let Jewels talk me into this. The phone rings.

"Hello."

"Hi, this is Mike. I'm calling about your daughter."

"Which one, I have three?"

"I'm calling about Natalie."

"What she done got herself into some kind of trouble?"

"No, I thought you might want to know where she is living."

"To be honest, I really don't care."

"Are you sure about that?"

"Yes, I told Natalie if she was going to be a dike, she couldn't be one here."

"I'm sorry what did you say?"

"You heard me, my daughter likes girls."

"So you're going to disown her because of that?"

"Wouldn't you?"

"No, she's still your daughter no matter what. You should think about talking to her and see why or how this even started. You never know what she could be going through."

"I never thought about that."

"Here is my number. Anytime you want to talk to her please don't hesitate to call. She and my daughter Jewels will be going to LA for a week."

"Oh, you're Jewels's father. Your daughter is a sweet young lady. I don't know why Natalie couldn't be like her."

"I was always told never to compare yourself with anyone because you never know what that person has gone through to be who they are today. I'm so glad that you think highly of my daughter. I've seen some changes in your daughter since she's been living with us. I am surprised to hear you say that she likes girls. They've been trying to go out on dates."

"Are you sure? Maybe she's changed. Maybe my words helped with that."

"You should never give up on your child no matter what choices they make. I know I've made some crazy ones in my life and I'm glad my mother didn't give up on me."

"Thank you so much for calling. I was worried but my pride stopped me from looking for her."

"No problem. You have my number. Just call when you want to talk."

We hung up the phone and I started thinking about what she had said. I wonder why Jewels didn't tell me that Natalie liked girls. I wonder if Jewels like them too. Oh no, my daughter is gay. Please don't let her be. I've been through too much and I don't know how I'm going to handle this. I will talk to her about this later.

I can't believe it. Jewels is going to be gone from me for a whole week. It's been a while since we have been separated. I had to ask Jewels about the gay thing. I've been carrying this on my mind for too long. I called Jewels into my room to tell her that I had spoken to Natalie's mother and she was real nice. She started smiling and saying I don't have to cook for you. She wipes her hand across her forehead showing a sign of relief.

I asked her if Natalie was gay. She looked at me and said, "Not anymore."

"What do you mean not anymore?" I asked.

She sat on my bed and said, "I didn't know that Natalie was gay at first and when I found out, I was already her friend. I didn't want to stop being her friend because she likes girls. If it wasn't for her next-door neighbor I don't think she would be."

"What do you mean?" I asked.

She started telling me how the neighbor's daughter has been messing with her. I couldn't believe it. "Don't worry, Dad, I still like boys," she says. I never thought I would be happy to hear her say those words. That's one less thing I have to worry about. I grabbed her and gave her a hug. I looked up at the ceiling and said, "Thank you, God."

"Jewels, hurry up and get through packing so I can take you and Natalie to the airport. You know you still owe me dinner since you decided to keep that piece of important information from me."

"Daddy, that's not fair."

"Baby, life isn't fair. Now hurry up before you miss the plane."

As I watch my daughter get ready to leave me for a week I realize how she has grown to be a beautiful, sweet young lady in spite of all the things she has been through. I'm so proud of her.

The phone rings and it was Natalie's mother. She wanted to talk to her before she went to LA. I told Jewels to pick up the phone.

What am I going to do while she is gone to my mother's, I thought. I guess I could use this time to work on that project at work. I can get my team together and do some kind of team builder with them. I will think of something to keep myself busy. As I look back over my life I can't do anything but rejoice on how good God has been to me. A CEO, I never thought I would have gotten this far.

I went to get the mail out the mailbox and I noticed a letter from my mother was there. I hope she's not telling me that Jewels can't come. I wonder why she didn't call to let us know that. I opened it and it read.

Dear Jewels,

I really wasn't for sure if I should give this to you. I've had it for a while. I thought about it and knew if it were I, I would want to know that my mother was trying to reach out to me.

I can't wait to see you when you come down.

Mike, if you're reading this letter please do not keep it from Jewels. She really needs to know that her mother is thinking about her. I know how protective you are of her but you can't keep certain things away.

I love you both,
Momma

I opened up the other letter and it was from Tracie. Before I got to the first line, I was ready to throw it in the trash. How did my mother know? I called Jewels in my room and gave her the letter. She saw that it was from Tracie and she began to smile. I told her to wait until she got on the plane before she read the letter. She folded it up and put it in her back pocket. I couldn't believe Tracie had turned her life around. I'm so glad and I know Jewels would be happy to hear that. I hope this won't change Jewels's attitude. I packed their things into the car and we were on our way to the airport.

Seeing her get on the airplane made me realize how much I love her and how much I'm going to miss not having her around. I'm glad that her friend came with her so she didn't have to fly alone. I drove off thinking about the letter that Tracie had sent and I really wanted to hear her voice. I think I will give her a call when I get to the house. Even though our relationship didn't work out I still want the best for her.

I pulled into the driveway and I noticed that a package was at the door. I looked at it and it said, "To Mike from Sade." I'm wondering what this could be. I took it into the house and opened it. To my surprise, it was a ticket to Vegas for a week. I was really shocked and then the doorbell rings. *Who could this be?* I thought. I opened it up and it was Sade. A smile came across my face. I was really happy to see her. She walked in and boy did she look fine.

"So I guess Jewels is gone," she says.

"Yes."

"So that means you are here all by yourself."

"Yes."

"Do you have plans?"

"No."

"Why all the short answers?"

"I don't know. I'm just surprised to see you."

"Is that a good thing or a bad thing?"

"Oh it's a good thing."

"Do you want to accompany me to Vegas?"

"I would love to. The plane doesn't leave until tomorrow."

"That's right."

"So what do you want to do until then?"

"You tell me," she said.

"Well, I've tivoed the game, do you want to sit and watch it?"

"Excuse me, you did what?"

"Sade, you know I'm just messing with you. I wanted to see what your reaction was going to be. Anything you want it's all up to you."

"Anything?" she said.

"Yes, anything."

She grabbed me and began kissing me. I was shocked. I think she had this whole thing planned. I was cool with that. I picked her up and carried her into the bedroom.

The Letter

Jewels

"I can't believe my mother wrote me."

"Well tell me, what does the letter say?"

"Natalie, I'm really scared to read it. Will you read it for me?"

"Sure."

"No, that's okay. I'll do it."

"Are you sure?"

"Yep, I want to do it. I'll let you know what it says when I finish."

"Cool."

The memories I had blocked out of my mind just so I could move on with my life begin to come back up as I started to read the letter. I was so glad to read that she was doing better and that she had changed her life, but I'm still wondering why it had to take her so long and what I did to deserve the pain that I had to endure for those years.

I thought my feeling would be different if I heard from her but it's not. Her apology doesn't stop the pain and it can't erase the memories. I wonder if I should call her when I get to grandmother's. How could she think that money would make things better? Who in their right mind would think that way? My grandmother should have burned this letter when she got it.

"So what does it say?"

"Oh nothing," I said. "She is just apologizing to me about how things went. She said that she has turned her life around and that she's in church now and wants to see me."

"That's good. You should see her while we're there."

"Natalie, I don't know if I really want to see my mother. Just reading the letter pulled out some bad memories. I might not be able to control my anger."

"If you don't you will always wonder in the back of your mind what if and that will haunt you more than knowing."

"You might be right."

"Jewels, you have been a blessing to me and I know I've said this so many times. You opened up your doors to your home and your heart as a friend and I really appreciate that. And now it's time for you to help yourself. If you don't find closure now all the whys will be with you for the rest of your life."

"You're right, Natalie. I know it's going to be hard but I have to do it."

"A part of me is happy that my mom wrote. Now I know that she's sorry for what she's done and that she really cares about me. I really thought she didn't. I wonder how she looks. The last time I saw her she didn't look too good. My mother has changed her life around. That's good, I just hope she doesn't go back to her old ways."

I leaned back in my chair, laid my head down, and closed my eyes. I began thinking about the letter that my mother wrote. Before I knew it Natalie was waking me up telling me that we were there. My heart started beating fast with excitement. I couldn't wait to see my grandmother's face. I walked down the terminal and there she was waiting on me. I ran into my grandmother's arms and hugged her tight.

I didn't want Natalie to feel left out so I invited her into the hug. My grandmother is so sweet. She treats everyone like they are a part of the family, well everyone except my mother. I still don't know why they don't get along. I thank grandmother for letting us come here and we went to baggage claim to get our bags.

As we were on our way to her house the scenery reminded me of the old days when granny and I used to go for rides around the city. We passed the hospital that my mom was taken to the night that

I found her lying on the floor. Anger started to sit in quickly. It was a feeling that I couldn't get a hold of. Then I saw him, the man that stripped me from my innocence. I tried hard to hold back the tears but I couldn't. Natalie looks at me and asks if everything was all right. I told her that my allergies were starting to bother me.

As we turned the corner to go to my grandmother's house all I could think about is what I would do to him if I ran into him again. I got out of the car and ran into the house. As I went into the living room I heard a familiar voice call out my name. It was my mother. I ran into her arms and hugged her tight. I never thought this day would have come. She looked so beautiful. I can tell that she has been taking care of herself.

I gave my grandmother a weird look. She smiled and whispered, "I did it for you, Angel."

I smiled and said, "Thank you." I introduced Natalie to my mother and we went upstairs to put our things down. I told Natalie that I needed to talk to my mother alone and that she could hang with my grandmother if she didn't mind.

"Girl, go handle your business," she said. "Your grandmother has already made me feel welcome."

My mom and I went to the guest room of my grandmother's house. She kept staring at me. I was wondering what was going on in her mind and then she said, "I'm sorry. I'm sorry that you had to go through those things."

"Why, Momma, why did you hate me so?"

"I didn't hate you. I just didn't know how to love you."

"What are you talking about?"

"Jewels, no one ever showed me how to love someone else. I always had things my way. I never had to do anything for anyone until I met Daddy."

"Why did you bring his name up? I just saw him walking down the street."

"Well, when your daddy and I decided to go our separate ways after he left high school, I met Daddy. I didn't know he was a pimp when I met him. He forced me to do things that weren't right. No one ever told me that what he was doing to me was wrong so when he did it to you I thought that was normal. Later after I went to counseling I found out that my stepdaddy molested me and some of that contributed to the choices that I had made in my life."

"Momma, I didn't know that you went through so much as a child."

"How would you have known? Your father doesn't know. I found the Lord and he helped me release the anger that I had inside and he also showed me that every person that come in and out of your life, we pull from them or they pull from us. And the things that we pull from them can be good or bad. As I was going through my reconstruction I noticed all the different personalities that I had pulled from all these different people that passed my way and none of them was who God had wanted me to be."

"I'm glad that you've gotten yourself together but it's hard for me not to forget. I had nightmares for days and your verbal abuse still haunts me. As I sit here listening to you the anger inside is building up more and more and I don't understand why. My mind is wondering why everything is going well with you. All this time I thought I was over it but now that I'm here I realized I had only blocked the pain and the anger out of my mind."

"I hate that you had to go through those things and I wish I could take them back but I can't. I've made some bad choices in my life and all I can do is focus on the now and I'm more cautious of the choices that I make."

"My mind and heart is so confused. I was happy to find out that you wrote me and was more excited to hear your voice and see your face but now as I look at you all I can remember are the words that you used to say to me and how you watched that man rape me and deny that it happened. You turned your back on me, treated me like I was trash, and told me that I would never amount to anything. You didn't call me on my birthday and now that you have turned your life around and found God you think everything is going to be all right."

"Jewels, I can't tell you enough how much it hurts me but I can't change what happened."

"Why not, why can't you change it? Because of you I'm scared to talk to boys. Because of you I really don't know how to open up and express how I really feel because I don't know if they really want to talk to me or if they just want my body. I always wonder in the back of my mind if this is some boy that my mother has set up. You don't understand how hard it's been without having you in my life. All I wanted you to do is love me, hug me, give me kisses, and tell me how much you appreciated me. But instead of that I got nothing but negative words. You never spent time with me. I really can't remember a day you read a book to me or helped me with my homework. All those memories that I have are from my daddy and my grandmother. How can you live with me and don't have any love for me? How can you carry me for nine months and give birth to me and don't provide protection for me? How can you look me in my face and tell me that if it wasn't for my daddy I would have been dead? How could you? I really thought I could do this.

"I really thought that I had forgiven you for all those things that you've done to me but I haven't. I guess I'm going to need God to intervene into my life like he did yours and turn my life around, because right now all I feel is hate for you and that man you call Daddy. I'm feeling that revenge needs to take place and I just don't know how I want it to happen."

"Jewels, please you're scaring me. I've never seen this side of you before. What's been going on in Dallas?"

"Dallas has nothing to do with the way that I am feeling right now, Tracie. All these feelings were bound on the inside and I didn't realize it until now. LA has so many bad memories for me, and seeing that Daddy guy stirred up a lot of it before I saw you. All I ever wanted was a relationship with you and now I'm not sure if I will ever be able to forgive you."

"Jewels, I think you and I need to go to counseling so we can work on our relationship. I've been praying that we could work things out and I really believe that we can. Please tell me that you will think about it."

"I really don't want to say. I have your number. I will call you, don't call me."

I walked out of the room very confused. How did this happen? All this time I wanted a relationship with my mother and now that she's here it's like it really doesn't matter if we have one.

"How did it go?" Natalie asks.

"Not too well."

"What happened?"

"I really don't know. I snapped."

"What do you mean you snapped?"

"She started talking and I starting thinking about all the things that I went through and anger set in. I mean I kept asking her how she could allow all those things to happen to me. She told me about what happened to her when she was younger. That made it worse because I started thinking if she went through all this why wouldn't she be overprotective of me and make sure that those things didn't happen to me?"

"Jewels, if she apologized the least you could do is forgive her."

"I don't know if I can, if I do it's like I'm forgetting that it ever happened and saying that it was okay."

"I don't think that's true. You can forgive without forgetting. I know there are some choices that I've made that I would want forgiveness for. I can't tell you what to do but I just hope you make the right decision."

"I don't know. What a way to start my vacation. I prefer not to talk about it right now. We should be having fun."

"Okay, whatever you say."

My grandmother didn't ask me anything about what my mother and I talked about. I know she's waiting on me to say something.

"Jewels, telephone."

My grandmother yells up the stairs. I hope this isn't her calling me.

"Hello."

"Hey, Angel, how was the flight?"

"It was fine, sorry I didn't call you when I got in. My mother was here."

"She was? I know she was happy to see you."

"Yeah she was. I was happy to see her too but then I started thinking about what happened and I snapped."

"I can't tell you how to feel, Baby, but you're going to have to forgive her in order to move forward in your life."

"Why do I have to forgive her? If I do that's making it seem like everything that she allowed to happen to me was okay."

"No, Jewels, forgiving her is allowing you to have closure to that part of your life, as long as you continue to harvest so much anger on the inside against your mother that part of your life will haunt you forever. Just think about it and don't allow this to ruin your vacation."

"I won't."

"I love you, Angel."

"I love you too, Daddy."

My daddy always has a way of making everything okay. He has so much compassion in his words, and I know if he was able to forgive her I should be able to do the same.

Forgiveness

Tracie

It wasn't supposed to happen this way. I did all this for her and she didn't appreciate any of it. What else can I do? Lord, I know what I did was wrong and I have admitted and apologized for it over and over again but it seems as if it's not enough. What else? Maybe our relationship is not supposed to be. I should just leave well enough alone. As I was walking out of Mike's mom's house, Momma Agnes called me into her room. "What's going on?" she asked.

"I don't get it. I've tried my best to get myself together so I could be the type of mother that Jewels need and she doesn't want it. She is so angry and full of hate. I could tell by the look in her eyes."

"You have to give her time. It took you over a year to get yourself together and you want everything to be okay with the two of you in a day. Just imagine how she's been feeling all this time. It wouldn't be so hard if you had tried to keep in touch. I can remember days when Mike couldn't get Jewels out of the room. He would call and ask me what he should do. It's been a hard road for the both of them and now you have to wait until they're ready. Don't give up. God has pulled you out for a reason so stay focused and pray that he will pull Jewels out as well."

"Thank you so much, Momma Agnes. I want to tell you how sorry I am for treating you the way I did. I was still a child in an adult's body not knowing how a lady is supposed to act. I want to thank you for all the help that you gave to me when I was pregnant with Jewels and after she was born."

"You are so welcome. I forgive you and I want to apologize to you as well because there were times when I acted out of character and I shouldn't have. You just continue to keep God first and know that it's all in God's plan and if it's meant for you and Jewels to have a relationship it will happen. Just don't try to move too fast because that can determine the overall outcome."

"Thanks, I love you."

"I love you too."

The talk with Momma Agnes helped a lot. I was really discouraged when Jewels walked out of that room. Now I know there is hope. I got to the house and laid my head on the pillow. As soon as I closed my eyes, there was a knock on the door. I wonder who this could be. I opened the door and there he was as fine as he could be. This tall black man with muscle everywhere possible is standing at my front door. He smells so good Lord knows I don't need this right now. I'm trying to stay calm. It's been almost two years since I touched a man and my hormones is ready to attack him. I noticed my hands trying to creep toward his chest. I snatched them back and pop them.

"Hello, how may I help you?"

"Hey I'm your new neighbor. I'm sorry to be knocking at your door like this but I have locked myself out of my place and I need to use the phone to call my roommate."

"One moment, let me get the cordless phone. My momma told me to never let a stranger into your home."

Roommate, oh Lord I hope this man is not gay. Please tell me this man is not gay, I thought.

"I do understand that," he said.

"Here you go just knock on the door when you've finish."

As I closed the door, I pressed my ears to the door hoping to find out if he was going to call some partner of his. "Hey, man, this is Mark," I hear him say. "I need for you to come back. I lost my key, yeah I know this is a special day for you and your girl but I'm sitting outside half-dressed with a towel over my body using the neighbor's phone… Thirty minutes, what am I going to do for thirty minutes? All right I will be at the pool, if not just hit me back on this number."

My number, how is the man going to tell somebody to call him back on my number? He doesn't know me like that. He knocks on the door. "Oh are you done?"

"Yeah and thanks," he said. "Oh my roommate said it's going to be about thirty more minutes before he will be able to bring me the key. I told him to call back on this number if he didn't see me at the pool. I hope you don't mind."

"Well, if I did it's too late now. Do you want to hang here for a while until your friend comes?"

"I thought your mom said not to let strangers into your home."

"She did, but what she doesn't know won't hurt her. This will be our little secret. Would you like something to drink?"

"A glass of water would be fine."

Could this be the one? Tracie girl, hush, you don't even know this man. My hormones are going wild. Why did he have to knock on my door half-dressed with water dripping all over his body?

"Are you hot?" I asked.

"No I'm fine, but as you can see I don't have that much on."

"Yea I noticed, so how long have you been living in LA?"

"I just moved out here. That's why I'm staying with my friend. He is going to propose to his ole lady on today and they should be moving to her place soon. So I'm going to be staying here until I can get myself together."

"So what made you move?"

"Change, I wanted to see some new scenery."

"Well you picked the right place for that."

"And I also want to be a rapper."

Oh Lord, not another rapper, I thought. "Oh really, I say."

"Yea I've been rapping for quite some time now but it hasn't popped off like I want it to."

"LA is the place to get famous. I wish you well."

"Thanks."

Why did he have to say a rapper? Ain't nothing wrong with wanting to be a rapper, it just seems like every black man I run into want to be in the entertainment business. Can a sista run into some black lawyers or doctors? There was a knock on the door. It was his friend. He told me that he would talk to me later. I thought, *What does that mean?* I looked at him and said okay and closed the door.

I lay back down on the bed hoping to get a quick nap and then the phone rings. Who can this be? Why is it that every time I try to lie down and get my thoughts together I get interrupted? "Hello." Oh well I'm not going to get any rest now. "Yes, Momma."

"I was wondering if you could come and pick me up and take me to get my medicine."

"Momma, where is your next-door neighbor?"

"She's gone and I don't want to wait."

"Momma, are you sure this can't wait until tomorrow, I really need to get some rest, because I'm working the night shift today?"

"Oh really, baby, I didn't know, well I guess it can wait. I'll see if my neighbor will take me."

"I thought you said that she wasn't there."

"Oh yea that's right. Well she should be back soon. I don't have to take another one until tomorrow morning anyway."

"Well let me know if she doesn't take you and I will stop by on my way home from work."

"Okay, baby, oh yea your aunt Rosie is coming down and she wants to see you."

"Let me know when she gets in. I have to go now."

"You be careful, it supposed to rain tonight."

"Okay, Momma. I think I will be okay. I will talk to you tomorrow."

"Okay, baby, Momma loves you."

"I love you too, momma."

My momma, sometimes I wonder if she's taking too much medication. She doesn't remember half of the stuff that she tells me and I bet you she doesn't need any medicine. I remember one day she called me frantic about her medication and how she's running low and she needed to get it filled that day. I went over there and that woman had a brand-new bottle sitting on her dresser. I was mad but what can I say, that's my momma.

I finally decided to turn my ringer off and close my bedroom door. This was going to be the only way I would get some sleep. My alarm clock went off at 5:00 p.m. and I was dragging. I turned on the shower and let the water fall on my face hoping that it will wake me up and then there was a knock on the door. Where is all this traffic coming from? I haven't had all this in and out since I left that house. I ran to the door and it was Mark. Now here I am with only a towel wrapped around my body dripping with water.

"Now this is the way a man wants to be greeted," he said.

"Don't get your hopes up. My momma said—"

"The last time you told me what your momma said, you turned around and said what she doesn't know won't hurt her, so is this going to be the case?"

My mind was telling me no, but my body was saying yes, yes, yes. "No that won't be the case," I said. "I do have my boundaries."

"I'm glad to hear that. Well I think I left my wallet on your couch. Can you check for me?"

Don't tell me this man left his wallet and I didn't get a chance to be nosey. Oh well. Here it is right in my face. I was too busy feeling all warm on the inside I couldn't see it. I could have had the low down on this man. Oh well maybe next time.

"Here it is."

"So did you write all my information down?"

"I didn't know it was here. After you left I went to bed."

"So what you're saying is, if you did know you would have looked."

"I'm not saying anything. If you don't mind. I'm getting kind of cold and I need to get ready for work."

"Is this your way of saying 'get out'?"

"Yes and no. I really have to get ready for work and I don't want to be late. I must say you are a very interesting person and I wouldn't mind getting to know you more."

Did I just say that? This man is going to think I'm desperate. It's too late to turn back now.

"Oh you want to get to know me more. I like a woman who knows what she wants. I'll let you go. I guess you want my phone number?"

"No that's okay. I know where you stay."

He smiled and walked out the door. I can't believe what I just did. What's done is done. It's five thirty. I'm going to be late for work. I ran and got dressed and walked out of the door.

Falling in Love

Mike

I think I'm falling in love with Sade. She's making me feel like a man should feel. I really like it when she's lying next to me when I go to sleep and when I wake up. Seeing her beautiful face when I wake up makes my day. I never thought someone would be able to make me feel this way besides Tracie. "How did you sleep?" she asked.

"Fine."

"We need to hurry up so we won't miss our flight."

"I forgot all about us going to Vegas. I need to pack. How long will we be out there?"

"Our plane is scheduled to come back on Thursday."

"That's cool. Jewels is scheduled to come back Saturday."

She walks out of the room as I get up to pack. I hope I'm not moving too fast with her. I would hate to fall in love only to get hurt again. She had a limo service pick us up from the house to take us to the airport. This was the first time that I had ever had someone planned something for me like this. This felt real good and I love it.

The flight was smooth. We got our things and went to the hotel. Our room was on the eighth floor. They called it the president suite. She had candles lit and soft music playing in the background. Is this lady trying to get me whipped or what? I went to put my things down and notice the Jacuzzi was full of bubbles. I was ready but I kept my cool. I didn't want to mess up what she already had planned.

"You like it?" she asked.

"I love it."

"I thought you needed something to relax your mind. I know with all the changes that have come your way and how you've been worried about Jewels and all, I wanted to help release some of the tension."

"Sade, you just don't know how much I appreciate this. It's hard trying to be so hard and together all the time. You know that's a lot of pressure for a man, but I try."

"You don't have to be hard in front of me. I know you're all man and we all have to break down sometime."

She starts to rub my back and I close my eyes. Her voice just puts me in a trance. Then she began to rub my head and my eyes popped opened. All I could think about is Tracie. Tracie used to always rub my head when she knew I had a lot on my mind. I started feeling a little distant. This can't be happening. I don't need to be with anyone who reminds me of Tracie so I got up.

"Is everything okay?" she asked.

"Yeah I'm fine I'm starting to get a little hungry."

"Would you like for me to call room service?"

"Sure, order whatever you like. I'll eat it."

"Okay."

I laid down on the big king-size bed thinking about Tracie, wondering if I was really over her. She was my high school sweetheart and we promised that we would never separate from each other again. *What am I doing? I have this fine woman doing all this for me and I'm thinking about Tracie, the one who—*

"They said the food should be here in about thirty minutes," she said.

"Okay, what did you order?"

"I ordered some pancakes with sausage, a fruit tray, and some juice."

"That's sounds good. I can't wait."

"Mike. I know I've told you this so many times but I just can't help it, you are a wonderful man. I admire the way you have kept yourself together for your daughter, and the strength and confidence that you have inside turns me on. You are the one that I would love to live the rest of my life with."

Why did she say that? Together forever was the promise Tracie and I made. I couldn't do anything but look at her. I can't believe that I'm starting to feel a little bit uncomfortable. I never realized how much she reminded me of Tracie until now. Is this possible? Can this be right? Maybe coming here was a bad idea.

The food came and it looked good. She sat down next to me and began feeding me some pineapples. What was this woman trying to do? Why couldn't Tracie be like this? I looked at her and told her to stop.

"What's wrong?" she asked.

"Why are you doing this? This seems too good to be true."

"Why can't you just receive some good for a change? You're always doing for others. I'm here to serve you."

"Serve me, I don't get it. It's been a long time since someone has done that and it's hard for me to receive it. The only person who has served me was my mother and she stopped."

"Well it's time for her to pass the torch to the woman you will call your wife. I can't believe that I'm here trying to ease your stress and you're pushing me away. Why, Mike? Is there something going on that I need to know about?"

"Sade, something that you did reminded me of my ex-wife."

"Oh really."

"Yeah and it seemed weird."

"Well, Mike, I'm not your ex-wife. It's time for you to let that go, especially if you want to move on with your life."

"Who said that I wanted to move on?"

"Excuse me. So what are you saying? Was this some kind of rebound thing?"

"No, don't look at it like that"

"How else am I supposed to look at it? You came over to my house the night after you found out your ex was a prostitute crying in my arms telling me that you can't take it anymore and that you're through with her. Mike, you came to me. You know how I feel about you and if that's not the way you feel about me then we need to end this now. I'm too old to play mind games."

"Sade. I'm not trying to play any games with you. I really do think that you are a wonderful person…"

"But."

"But, before I commit myself to you I want to make sure that what Tracie and I have is really over. When I left, it was out of anger and hurt. When you touched me I want to think about you and not Tracie and right now I can't say that I don't."

"So where do we go from here?"

"Let's continue with our trip and enjoy ourselves. I want to have a talk with Tracie just to release myself from her."

"Are you sure that's what you want to do? Do you really want to release yourself from her or are you hoping that you two can get back together?"

"I don't know."

She walks out of the bedroom into the bathroom. I hope I did the right thing. I don't know. I really care for her but I want to make sure I'm not using her as a rebound. Sade is too good and she needs a good man in her life. I know that I'm a good man, but I just want to make sure that I can give her all of my heart and right now I don't think that I can. Reading that note from Tracie gave me a little hope. I don't know why I still have feelings for her, but I do. We've been through so much together. We have so many memories good and bad and I don't want to let them go to waste if I can help it. Why didn't I wait until after the week was over? I wonder what kind of week this is going to be. I know I can kiss the sex good-bye. Why would she want to give me some after what I just said?

Someone for Me

Sade

I can't believe this. How can this man look me in my face and tell me that he is still thinking about his ex. After all that I have done to make this week feel special for him. I hope he doesn't think he's going to get some because the doors are closed at Sade's.

When am I going to find someone for me? I've been waiting for so long to find that special person and when I thought I found him his heart is not with me but with someone else. When will I get my chance to experience true love? I'm almost thirty and I don't have any kids. Ever since I was a little girl I always dreamed that I would be a wife and a mother before I reached thirty and I don't think that's going to happen. I worked hard to make sure that I was wife material and all that hard work has not paid off. Mike is a good man. I know in my heart that he is the man for me. What did that woman do to him? Am I trying too hard or something? I thought every man wanted to be catered to but I guess I was wrong.

Four more days with this man and we can go our separate ways. I might as well enjoy it because I really don't know when someone else is going to come my way. Man, why me? Oh this water feels so good all I need now is a glass of champagne. Why don't I tease him just for a minute? "Mike!" I yelled out.

"Yeah."

"Will you please bring a glass of wine?"

"All right."

He walks in and begins to smile. "Here you go," he said.

"Thanks." He kept staring at me and I can tell by the look on his face he wanted to join me and that's the look I wanted to see. I knew he would come around. Why am I doing this to myself? He has already told me that he wasn't for sure if I was the one. He bends down in front of the tub, and asks if I want him to wash my back. I guess he wasn't thinking about Miss Tracie. I looked up and said, "Sure." Oh his hands feel so strong and all I could do was think about how good he feels inside of me. I want him and I don't care about that stuff he said. I believe he's the one and I'm going to act like he is. He got in the tub with me and began kissing me on my neck. I'm going to whip it on him so good that he won't know how to spell her name. I took a sip of the wine and relaxed myself on him. It was feeling so good that my eyes started rolling to the back of my head.

I could tell he was enjoying every move I made by the expressions on his face. The sweat started dripping down his face to his neck from the warm water and that made him look even more delicious. I had to prove to him that Tracie was not the one and this was the only way. I always said that I would never be the woman on the other side but now I'm wondering if I would leave him alone if he chose Tracie.

The beautiful sun coming in from the window woke me up. I turned and noticed that Mike was not in the bed. I called out his name and he didn't answer. I wondered where he could have gone. I went into the bathroom to wash my face and all I could do was think about last night. Last night was better than all the other nights that we have had together. I think I'm falling in love with him and I'm so mad at myself because I know that he might end up going back to his ex-wife. I can't let this happen.

"Sade." I hear him say.

"I'm in the bathroom." I walk out and there he was standing there with a dozen of roses. I couldn't do anything but smile. He looked into my eyes and said he was sorry about last night. He shouldn't have ruined the trip with his feelings of Tracie. He told me how much he appreciated all that I have done for him and that he really want to try and make this work.

"What about Tracie?" I asked.

"I still want to talk to her since I haven't had a chance to speak with her since we divorced," he said.

"I hope you're not trying to tease me."

"Sade, there's something about you that give me a sense of peace. When I woke up this morning, I stared at you for a long time. You look so beautiful in your sleep. I kept asking myself why. Why am I treating you like this? You have been there for me when no one else was there. You help me get through a rough part of my life. I started thinking about the things that I said to you and the things that has happened to me in the past. I was as shocked as you were when I noticed that you did something that reminded me of Tracie but I shouldn't have pushed you away like I did. I really care for you, Sade, and that's why I want to be nothing but honest with you."

"I'm glad that you want to be honest and I think it will be a good idea if you did speak with Tracie. Mike, let's enjoy the remaining days that we have left and finish this conversation when we get back to Dallas."

"You're right."

His words brought peace to my mind. I just pray that he isn't running game on me. Las Vegas is so nice. I've been here before but it's so much better when you go with someone you like. I lost about five hundred dollars on the card table but it was cool. Mike picked up about two thousand. He felt bad for me and gave me the five hundred of his winnings. I thought that was so sweet of him.

We did the four in one Canyon County. That's when you tour the Grand Canyon by airplane, bus, boat, and then by helicopter; the view from all different angels were beautiful. I could get used to being with Mike and traveling to different places. Mike made me feel special in spite of all the things he said the other night. It felt like a real relationship to me. I can't wait to see the pictures that we took together.

I wonder how Jewels is going to react to me. I know she's been through so much with her mom, and she might not want another woman to come into their lives. How can I get her to like me? I want so much for this to work. I think I can show her so many different things.

I've never been involved with a guy who have kids. I know it has to be hard work. I can't think about this right now. I have to enjoy the moment at hand.

When we got back to the hotel Mike had the room lit with candles. He had rose petals leading to the bedroom. I followed the rose petals into the bedroom and it ended with a bed full of roses. On the nightstand, he had an ice bucket with a bottle of wine in it and a fruit tray.

"When did you arrange this?" I asked.

"Don't you worry about that, let's just enjoy this moment."

"Okay, so what do you have planned?"

"Not sex if that's what you are thinking."

"Who said I was thinking about sex?"

"I just want us to enjoy each other's company. I want to make sure that what we have is not just sex. Every time that we have been together, we ended up taking our clothes off and I don't want to do that this time."

Why did he say that? How is he going to set a romantic scene and don't want to get romantic. He knows he's real wrong for this one. Oh well you don't always have to have sex even though the scenery puts you in the mood for it.

"That's sounds good," I said.

"I'm glad you think so now lay down and let me cater to you. You've been catering to me so much and now I want to return the pleasure."

Hold up. This man is about to rub all over me and I know he doesn't think I'm not going to want to have sex. Why is he doing this to me? I guess he is trying to get me back from last night. I turned on my stomach and the minute he touched my back I thought about last night. My hormones starting going crazy but I kept my cool. I want to be like a wild woman but I keep focusing on being a lady. My mind began to feel so relaxed and my body followed. *This man has to be my husband, Lord, please make a way.*

After he finished massaging my body, we laid there in bed talking about our feelings. He told me about the letter that Tracie wrote to Jewels and he thinks that's how all those feelings of her arose. He told me that he thinks he's falling in love with me but he's apprehensive because he doesn't want to get hurt. I told him that I wasn't here to hurt his heart but to help mend it. He told me how he prayed to God that he will send the right woman into his life and that he believes that I am that woman.

His words were making me fall more and more into him. Even though we weren't having intercourse I felt like we were. I never laid down with a man and just cuddled. If we laid down it was to have sex or to go to sleep.

Mike has taken this relationship to a whole new level and I thank God for it.

Flashback

Jewels

I wonder where my dad could be. He's not answering the home phone or his mobile. I hope nothing has happened to him. I went into my grandmother's room to ask her if she had heard from him and she said that he went out of town and will be out of pocket until Thursday. How dare he go out of town and not tell me. It must have been a last-minute business trip. Oh well, I really wanted to talk to him about the incident with my mother. I guess it will have to wait until I get back. My grandmother asked Natalie and me to go to the store to get a loaf of bread, two cans of peaches, and some more things.

Natalie and I started walking to the store and I would tell her stories about different things that had happened to me. I had her crying, laughing. We got the things that she wanted and we were on our way back to my grandmother's house when we ran into that man—Daddy. I couldn't believe it. I didn't think I would see him so soon. I just got here and my past keeps coming from every angle. He walked up to me and said, "Haven't I seen you somewhere before?"

"What do you mean? You don't remember? I was the little girl that you raped."

"Raped? I don't know what you are talking about."

"You don't remember Diamond?"

"Oh yeah now I remember, where is Diamond, I haven't seen her in a while?"

"Don't you think you owe me an apology for the things that you did to me?"

"Little momma, that was the past so get over it. You know you liked it."

Before I knew it, I kicked him in his balls and he fell on the ground. Something inside of me said, "Kill him." He deserves to die for all the things that he has done to you. I started kicking him all over. I started stomping him in his face and back. Natalie began to scream, "Stop you're killing him." I turned around with tears falling down my face and said, "He must feel the same pain that I feel. He must be humiliated just like I was." I started beating him with the grocery bag and blood started coming out of his nose. I wanted him dead. The anger and pain that I thought I was over all came back in tenfold. I can hear Natalie screaming in the background but something inside of me kept telling me to keep going. I started kicking him more in his balls. If I had a knife I think I would have chopped them off. I heard Natalie say, "He's not moving." At that moment I stopped and looked at him, his face was full of blood, and he wasn't moving. Did I kill him?

"I think he's dead," Natalie said.

"No he's not."

"How do you know? He's not moving."

"But he's still breathing."

"We better go, Jewels."

We started running toward my grandmother's house.

"Why did you do that? I never saw that side of you before in my life. It was like you were the devil or something," Natalie said.

"You wouldn't understand. There are a lot of things that you don't know about me. I tried to block them in the back of my head and I did for a while but coming here just brought them back."

"If it was so bad here then why did you want to come back?"

"You've met my grandmother. She's the sweetest person you could ever know. I needed to see her. I wanted to spend some time with her."

"Do you think he's coming to look for you?"

"I don't know and I don't care. He needs to be locked up or buried six feet under somewhere. If you hadn't stopped me he would have been on his way to his grave."

"I can't believe you are talking like this. I have never seen this side of you. You always showed compassion and love and now it's like you're full of rage and vengeance."

"That man raped me in front of my mother and then when I began to vomit he got up off of me and started peeing on me. Don't you know how hurt and humiliated I was? I bled for three days. I thought it was my period but it wasn't. He had ruptured a part of my insides. Luckily it healed up okay."

"Why didn't you tell me this before?"

"Natalie, I really didn't want to talk about it, would you? I mean I was so happy that I didn't have to worry about that part of my life anymore when I came to Dallas. All I wanted to do was look forward and not focus on the past."

As we were walking back to the house I couldn't help but think about what I just done. It felt so good. It was like I was releasing the pain that he had caused me, back on him. I wasn't for sure if my method was right but it seemed like it was right at the time. I guess my mother has let him go. I remember hearing him say that he hadn't talked or seen her in a while. Now I realize why my dad went to counseling. I think it's time for me to go and be honest with the counselor.

When I handed my grandmother the bag she gave me this crazy look and said, "Baby, what am I supposed to do with this?" I told her that I dropped it on our way back. She said, "That's fine." She didn't realize until after we left that she needed some more things at the store.

I couldn't believe that I lied to my grandmother. It came out so easy. I hope she never finds out about what happened. I don't know what she would think of me if she did.

Natalie has been a little distant with me today. I think she's still thinking about yesterday. I hope she doesn't start acting different now. After all I've been nothing but a true friend to her. When people wouldn't look at her or give her any attention I was there. I was the one who gave her the makeover so boys would give her the time of day. I hope she doesn't turn her back on me. If she does that means she wasn't a true friend anyway.

Opened Up

Natalie

They say the real you will soon come out in time. I can't believe Jewels have so much anger in her. I wonder what else is going on in her head that I'm not aware of. I've come to realize that people are living actors and actresses who play dress up to be who they think other people want them to be, instead of finding out who they are and being themselves.

I thought I was going through hard times but it seems as if Jewels is going through some things in her life as well. I don't know if she is the friend I thought she was. All this time I was sharing my life with her and she never really opened up her life to me. She never told me she was molested until now. I wonder why she didn't tell me. Oh well I know if I mention something to her now she's going to get all upset so I guess I will wait for her to come to me. I hope this is not how the rest of this trip is going to be. I could have stayed home if that was the case.

I wonder what my siblings are doing. It's been a while since I've spoken to them and I know my little sister Naomi is waiting on me to brush her hair like I use to. I was so glad when my mom called to talk to me and I know she will be happy to hear that I stopped messing with girls. I wonder if I should tell her about what the next-door neighbor's daughter did to me. She probably won't believe me if I did. Life can be so hard sometimes especially when you don't have all the answers. And with the answers that you think you have, you wonder how the outcome will turn with the choices that you make.

This trip was supposed to take my mind off things but it seems as if it has only gotten my mind thinking about a lot of other things. Now that I'm talking to boys I wonder if they're going to want to have sex with me. How will they act if I say no? I've never had sex and the thought of it scares me. And if I do it what if it's not good or the boy goes back to school and tell everyone that we did it. I can't take that type of humiliation in my life. I've already been humiliated by people calling me fag and dike. The last thing that I want to be called is a hoe. I can hear them saying, "You nasty hoe dike." I'm so mad at myself I can't believe I did those things with that girl. That's going to be with me for the rest of my life.

I stayed my distance from Jewels because I didn't know what she was thinking and I didn't want to say the wrong thing and then she snap and starts beating me. I wonder if he got up or if he died. I know she said that he was still breathing but the blood was coming down so fast from his face. I've never seen a person laid out on the ground with blood rolling down their face like his was. The thought of it makes my skin crawl.

When we got up the next morning I still kept my distance. I know she's wondering what was up with me but I'm not going to say anything until she does. While we were at the table the doorbell rang. Her grandmother answered it and it's the police. I couldn't believe it, the police was here looking for Jewels. They sat down and started talking about something but I couldn't hear. Jewels called me upstairs so I left and went with her.

"So why do you think they are here?" she asked.

"Maybe the man is dead and they're looking for the both of us because a witness saw me and you around him."

"No, no one likes him. Who would tell the cops on us? I bet they were happy that I was kicking his butt."

"You don't know that. Jewels, I'm not going to jail for what you did."

"So you're going to just leave me hanging like that. I thought we were friends?"

"We are friends but I'm too young to go to jail and that was not my problem that was yours."

"Oh, I see how you are. My problem, what about that night you came banging on my door because your mother had kicked you out of the house. That was not my issue but I was there for you."

"You're right but jail wasn't an option for you. A true friend wouldn't ask anybody to fall with them especially when that person didn't do anything."

"So you're saying that I'm not a true friend?"

"I'm not saying that you're not a true friend, Jewels, but what I am saying is that it's not right for you to ask me to fall with you. You should be asking me to be there to help and support you."

"You're right. I can't go to jail. Why should I be punished for what he did? He should be the one going to jail, not me. He raped me."

She begins to scream, "Why is this happening to me? What did I do to deserve this?" The person I thought had it all together was falling apart right before my very eyes and it was scary. She started pacing back and forth talking under her breath. I just stood there and watched for a moment and then I went down the stairs to see if the policemen were still there and they were gone. I walked downstairs where her grandmother was and she was pacing back and forth. I asked her what was wrong and she told me that her brother was in a car wreck and he died.

My heart dropped as the tears started falling down her face. All I could think to do was hug her. As I was hugging her, Jewels ran down the stairs. "What's wrong?" she asked.

"Your uncle died in a car wreck," I said.

"What uncle?"

"Your uncle Buddy," her grandmother said. "You never got a chance to meet him. He didn't come to California until after you left. He was my oldest brother. I told him not to be driving. The policeman said he thinks he blacked out and ran into a tree. I bet that's what happened because he was always doing that. Buddy was a stubborn old man who didn't want to listen to anybody."

"I'm sorry to hear that he died, Granny," Jewels said.

Her grandmother turned to her and said, "No need to say you sorry, Buddy is gone up to heaven now. He's watching over me just like my mother is. He's at peace now. I am sad that I won't see his physical body anymore but I am happy that his soul is with God."

"What do you mean his soul is with God?" I asked. She told us to sit on the couch and she grabbed her Bible and started reading 2 Corinthians 5:1-11. "God has a plan for all of us while we are here on earth," she says. "The first verse is using the words 'tent' and 'house' to represent our human body and once that is torn or no longer working our soul is released from the tent and goes up to heaven."

"I didn't know this," I said. "I wasn't aware that we were all here for a purpose."

"Everyone will not be able to serve his or her purpose," she said.

"Why not?" I asked.

"Not everyone knows or take the time out to find out what their purpose is."

"That sucks. How are we supposed to find out what our purpose is?" I asked.

"Only God knows and you will find out your purpose through him," she said.

My head is turning from everything that has happened while we have been here. I've heard about the word of God, but I never learned enough to understand what it's all about. What is my purpose? Wow, once you're dead your soul goes to the Lord, can this be true. I wonder if my mom knows this.

Death, pain, confusion, envy is this all a part of God? I don't know. I want to learn more about God and hopefully that will help me get myself together. I'm surprised that Jewels didn't say anything about what her grandmother was saying. I think she's thinking about the incident that happened on yesterday. I took a bold move and asked her what was on her mind.

"Nothing," she said.

"Are you sure?" I asked.

"Well, seeing the police really scared me. I thought that they were here for me and that my life was over. I know that what he did to me was wrong but if it came down to it how would I prove it to the judge. I don't know if my mother would testify against him especially since she was there watching everything when it happened. She might not want to get herself in trouble."

"That's a lot and I was scared for you. I hope you understand what I meant when I said that I couldn't go down with you."

"Yeah I must admit I was mad at first, but you're right you didn't have anything to do with it and I don't expect you to go down with me for that."

"I still don't understand why you didn't talk to me about all of this."

"I wanted to help you, Natalie. I didn't want you to feel sorry for me. My dad did enough of that all by himself. I felt that I could make myself feel better if I got my mind off of that and start keeping myself busy. Then I met you and I thought you would be the perfect person to keep me busy. I must admit at first I was using you so I wouldn't think about my problems and then when I got to know you and I realized you were a victim just like me, I started looking at you as a friend and not some project."

"We all have our reason for getting to know someone more. When I saw you I wanted to get with you so I had my own agenda. Then you made me realize that I can have a friend without me giving up myself and that if I wanted to be your friend I had to respect you as the person that you are and that's one who don't like girls in the way that I use to. Like I said before I've never had anyone show me any kind of respect so I didn't think that I was supposed to receive it. My mother talks to my siblings and me like we are on her level. She never had one man in her life for more than four months. So many different men were coming in and out of my life constantly and they had the nerve to want me to call them daddy.

"Then the next-door neighbor's daughter started messing with me and after that I didn't think I deserved respect at all from anyone.

I began feeling the same anger that you showed the other day and I was wondering why I didn't think to do that. Why didn't I go to the neighbor's daughter and start beating her until her face was full of blood. I just let it go like everything was okay. I showed my anger in other ways like snapping at my mom's male friends, drinking, and smoking."

"You and I are two different people, Natalie. It wasn't meant for you to react the way I did. I shouldn't have reacted in that way. It was as if I was being controlled by another force."

"Pain and anger, I've seen them make people burn up their own house because they found their mate cheating," I said.

"Yeah and how about breaking the windows off the new car?"

"And then there are others who get so angry that they hurt themselves. They commit suicide."

"You are so right about that. I was at a point in my life when I didn't want to live anymore. I wanted to cut myself with a knife, but fear sat in and I started thinking about how lonely my dad would be. I decided to be strong and bury the pain and anger deep down on the inside. It was hard but I had to do it."

Jewels and I talked all night until we went to sleep. I never felt so close to her like I do now. She opened up to me and I was happy. Now I can help her like she did me when I was in need. At first I was starting to regret the fact that I came but now I'm glad. Who would have thought I would have gained so much knowledge about life and emotions in two days.

Slip Up

Tracie

I can't believe I slept with Mark after knowing him for just a couple of days. I haven't had a man that close to me in about a year, I think. I know the Lord is not pleased with my actions but I fell weak to temptation. He was looking so good I had to taste him.

He's been coming by my place a lot since that night. I don't know what got into me. He came over and wanted to talk. We sat down and talked more about him wanting to be in the entertainment industry and how this had been his dream since he was a little boy. I couldn't do anything but stare at his sexy big arms. And the way he smelled took my mind to places I know it shouldn't have been. He had on Unforgivable.

As I was inhaling his scent I felt my body begin to twitch. I started moving around to make it go away but it wouldn't and before I knew it I jumped on him and started kissing his beautiful black lips. He pushed me back and said, "What about what your mother said?"

I looked at him and said, "Let's not talk about my mother right now."

He picked me up and took me to my room. I never figured out how he knew where my room was. Anyway he laid me on the bed and began to kiss me. My toes curled up and my eyes went to the back of my head. Before I knew it I was like a wild cat. I got up, threw him on the bed, and took control. His eyes got real big and then he closed them. He started making some crazy noises. It took a lot for me not to laugh. He was like, "Baby, give me more, faster, faster," and then he stopped.

"I know you're not finished," I said.

He looked up and said, "I don't know what got into me. You're the first person that has made me go that fast."

I couldn't believe it, the day that I decided to slip up it really wasn't worth slipping for. Maybe I just hyped myself up because he was so fine on the outside. I can honestly say that Mike did his thing when it came to the bedroom and I haven't found anyone better than him yet.

I haven't spoken to Jewels since the first day she came here. I really don't want her to leave on a bad note with me. I know that I'm the parent and I have to make the first move and I did that, so what else should I do. I picked up the phone and called her grandmother's house. She picks up.

"Hello," she said

"Hi, Jewels, this is your mother."

"Oh hey."

"I wanted to know if you wanted to hang out before you leave LA."

"I don't know. I have my friend Natalie with me and I don't want to leave her out."

"She's welcome to come with us. She doesn't have to be left out. I really think we need to put a closure to the pain that we both endured in the past."

"I really don't want to have that conversation while my friend is here."

"So when do you want to talk?"

"I don't know."

"Jewels, I've tried to be peaceful and patience. I'm still your mother and I think we need to have a talk about our relationship."

"Whatever."

"Don't use that tone with me. I will be over there in a couple of hours."

I know she just didn't hang up in my face. That girl has my attitude all the way. I'm determined to make this work between the two of us. I started getting ready to go see Jewels and the doorbell rings. I go to answer it and it's Mark.

"Hey, baby," he said.

"Hey, Mark."

"Well, I want to know if you want to go to the movies with me tonight."

"I'm sorry I can't today. I'm on my way out to see my daughter."

"You have a daughter?"

"Yes I do. She's here from out of town."

"I would love to meet her. Maybe we all can go to the movies together."

"Mark, I think it's too soon for all of that. Let's give it a few months."

"All right I'll call you tonight to see how everything went."

"Okay cool. I'm not sure what time I'll be home."

"Don't worry. I will wait up for you."

Wait up for me? We're not married what he needs to wait up for me for, I thought. With a smile, I looked at him and said, "Okay."

What have I started? Why didn't I keep my legs closed? I hope that I don't have a psycho on my hands. I closed the door and started to get ready. I noticed that my answering machine was blinking so I pushed the button to check it. The first call was my mother trying to go get her pain medications. I forward pass that and then I heard a familiar voice. It was Mike.

"Hey, Tracie, this is Mike. Jewels got your letter and I'm glad to hear that you are doing well. I really would like to hear from you. I'm out in Vegas and will be coming back on Thursday so when you get a free moment please give me a call. Our number is 214-555-5555. Jewels is staying over my mom's house, you should stop by and see her if you get a chance. Take care."

I wonder what he has to talk to me about. I bet he wants to get back with me since he knows that I've gotten myself together, I kind of miss ole Mike. *Tracie, don't get your hopes up too high. He might just want to say his good-byes*, I thought.

The machine beep to go to the next message and it was Daddy. How did he get this number? And what does he want from me.

"Hey, Diamond, I ran into your daughter the other day and she got me real good I must admit. I'm still in the hospital from the beating that she has done to me. I see how you want to play. The game has just begun. I should be out soon and when I do you better watch out."

If Jewels can put him in the hospital I know I can. I'm passed being scared of that man. Whenever he comes I'm ready. That Jewels, I wonder why she didn't tell me that she ran into him. I know he got what he deserves.

When I arrived at her grandmother's house everything seemed quiet. I know she didn't leave and she knew that I was on my way out here. I knocked on the door and she answered. "Come in," she said.

"Why such a long face?" I asked.

"No reason, I'm just tired of going back to the past. I really just want to look into the future and keep going from there."

"Me, too, but we can't if we allow our past to keep us in a holding tank. Where's your grandmother and friend?"

"They went to work out the funeral plans for Uncle Buddy."

"Your uncle Buddy died? I don't think you ever had a chance to meet him. He was a character. Your uncle Buddy could turn your frown into a big smile. I'm sorry to hear that he's dead. I will have to give her my condolences when I see her. So are you ready to talk?"

"Every time I think back on the things that have happened to me I get so angry. I know part of it is because of the pain and the other half is confusion. Still to this day no one has been able to tell me why. Why me? Why was I chosen to go through all of this pain? Why couldn't I be the one to live a stress-free life? I'm not even an adult yet and I've gone through so much. I hate to see what it will be like when I do become an adult."

"Life is challenging no matter what age group you fall under. I'm sorry but I can't answer your whys, I still haven't gotten the answers to mine. All I can do is pick up the pieces and put them back together again and ask God to help mend the wounds."

"This is all God's fault. If he has all this power why didn't he stop this from happening? Was me getting raped in his plans? If it was, how can you call that love and why would you ask him to help mend what he has broken?"

"Jewels, we can't blame God for everything that happens in this world. We have to take some ownership of our choices."

"You mean to tell me that I chose to get raped?"

"No, Jewels, that's not what I'm saying. All I'm saying is that we have a choice in life and sometimes the choices we make can affect other people. I made some bad choices and it trickled down to you and I'm sorry. I didn't think what I did in my life would have affected you in the way that it did."

"Why did you say you didn't want me? Don't you know how you made me feel? How would you feel if your mother didn't want you?"

"When I got pregnant with you I was still young. I was in college and my adult life had just started. I felt that having a baby would stop me from following my dreams and that's why I made that statement. I must admit and to think about it, it's sad to say but I was a little jealous of you. You took the only man who acknowledged me as a special person and who made me feel so important, away from me, and that person was your father. When you were born, he took one look at you and said "Jewels" and after that, I couldn't get him away from you. I wanted that, I had that and in the blink of an eye it was gone. I've learned a lot since I've been on my own. I didn't realize how much you meant to me until you left. I wanted to contact you but I also wanted to make sure that I had my life together before I called."

"I appreciate you being honest and I'm so happy that you really care about me. It was hard for me to accept the fact that you hated me and didn't want me. I really want us to be closer than we are but I don't want to rush into it because I'm scared that I'm going to get hurt again."

"I understand that and if I get to the point where I'm going too fast please let me know. I had my time with getting myself together and you deserve the same. I'm just glad to have you back in my life again. You've grown so much and you look so beautiful. I just realized how much you look like me when you smile. I don't mean to change the subject but I must ask what happened between you and Daddy."

"Are you talking about my daddy? Nothing has happened. I'm a little upset because he hadn't called to talk to me since the first night that I made it down here."

"No, not your father, I mean Daddy, the one who raped you. I got a voice message that you beat him up really bad and he's in the hospital."

"The hospital, well it's good to know that he's not dead I guess. Natalie and I saw him on our way back to Granny's house and he started talking and I flipped. Before I knew it I was kicking him in his private area and his head. I got so mad I took the bag of groceries and started hitting him on his legs and back. Natalie stopped me and we ran back here. The police came and I thought they were coming for me but they came to tell granny that Uncle Buddy had died. I don't know what got into me. All I felt was a burst of anger jumped out and I was ready to kill. It reminded me of the day when I started choking you. But my conscience didn't stop me with him like it did with you. It was kind of scary once I stopped and thought about what I did. I didn't have any control of my anger or my emotions."

"I'm not going to say that Daddy didn't deserve what he got but I do hate that you had to be the one to do it. When we keep all of our pain balled up on the inside all it does is grow until it explodes and that is what happened to you. You exploded and it almost caused a man's life. I know that's something you don't want to have on your conscience."

"So I was just supposed to let him get away with it?"

"I'm not saying that, but there is a better way that you could have handled it."

"Maybe you're right but at that time that's what I wanted to do. So what do you think he's going to do?

"Jewels, he's not going to do anything. Don't worry about him, he has no power over you or me. I have so much dirt on him that will put him in prison for life. Enough about him. Do you think we can amend our relationship? I know it's going to take some time."

"I think we can. So are you and my daddy going to get back together?"

"I don't know. He did call me and told me that he wanted to talk to me. He should be back from Vegas on tomorrow I think."

"He's in Vegas?"

"Yeah that's what he said on my machine."

"I am going to talk to him when I get home. He didn't tell me anything about Vegas."

"So are you his mother now?"

"No, he just tells me everything."

"Okay."

"Wow, I hope you two can get back together then it can be like old times. You can move to Dallas with us. The house is not as big as it was here but it's really nice. I'm so glad I came and we talked."

"Slow down. Your daddy and I have been divorce for a while now and he probably has gone on with his life."

"No, I don't think so. I mean he has a friend but I don't think they are serious. He hasn't told me that they were."

"We'll see. Don't get your hopes up too high."

I gave her a big hug and told her that I loved her and I left. I was so happy that everything turned out the way I wanted it. Now we can start over learning one another and becoming the mother and daughter that I always wanted. I wonder if Mike and I could get back together. He was my high school sweetheart and he is a good man. I can't wait until we talk.

I got to the house and sure enough, Mark was waiting. I really do think this man is a stalker. He asked me how my day went with my daughter and I said fine. He then asked me if I wanted to watch a movie with him. He had rented the *Diary of a Mad Black Woman*. I was surprised that he would have rented something like that, but he said he had seen some of Tyler Perry's plays and they were pretty good. He didn't get to see the movie when it was in theaters so he thought it would be cool to watch it with his new girl.

I stepped back and said, "What did you say?"

"My girl," he said.

"Mark, I think you're moving a little bit too fast for me. We just met. Let's get to know each other first before we start calling each other ours."

"So what you don't like me?" he asked.

"I think you're cool, it's just that I like to get to know a person before I start claiming them."

"You knew enough about me to have sex with me."

The man is talking like a woman. That's something I would have said. I guess I will answer like the man.

"Hey, Mark, I saw you and your body turned me own so I thought it would be nice to get to know you in that way. And I did."

"Was that the only reason?"

"Mark, you're scaring me. You're starting to sound too much like a woman."

"You don't have to worry about me in that department. I'm all man. I just thought you were a real nice woman and I really wanted to get to know you more and maybe start dating. The girls that I've been around have not been what I wanted."

"That's all you had to say. I don't have any problem with that but I do have one question."

"Go ahead."

"Do you always go that fast?"

"What?"

"Do you always go that fast?"

"I can explain. It had been over a year since I had sex. I used to be a real player and I decided to put down my cards and I made a commitment to myself that I wouldn't have sex with anyone else unless that person was real special to me. And when you attacked me my mind couldn't take it, I tried to hold out as long as I could, but you must admit you caught me off guard."

"Are you trying to say that it's my fault?"

"Partially yes, but I can't put it all on you. I would love to prove it to you."

"I bet you would but not right now."

"So, how about the movie, do you want to watch it?"

"Sure, why not."

I hope I made the right choice. I do understand how it is when you haven't had it in a while. That was the reason for me attacking him, but what about Mike. I don't want to get serious with Mark if I still have a chance with Mike.

I guess I won't know until we talk. Oh well I might as well enjoy this time with Mark just in case Mike is really serious with the friend that Jewels was talking about.

Grown Apart

Mike

I really enjoyed the trip with Sade. I didn't think I could have felt this way toward another woman. I know Jewels is going to be mad at me because I didn't call her. My mother's number was listed on the caller ID about thirty times. I wonder how she will feel when I tell her about my engagement with Sade.

I couldn't believe that I did it but my heart was telling me to. She is all I ever wanted in a woman. She's a self-starter, she's full of confidence, knows how to please a man, and she's beautiful. I couldn't let that go. I can still remember how her face looked when I asked her.

Jewels will be home tomorrow and I have to think of a way to tell her. Sade wanted to be here but I wasn't sure on how Jewels's response was going to be so I told her that I would do it by myself. With Sade and me together it will show Jewels how a positive relationship should be, and I know that will be the best thing for her.

The phone rang as I was unpacking my clothes, *I wonder who this could be*, I thought. I looked at the caller ID and it was my mom's number. "Hello," I said.

"Hey, Daddy."

"Jewels, I was just thinking about you."

"Where have you been? I've been calling like crazy."

"I know. I just finished looking at the caller ID. I went to Vegas with Sade."

"Oh, I didn't know you were going. Why didn't you tell me?"

114

"I didn't know either until I came back from taking you to the airport. Enough about me, how are things going out there?"

"It's fine. Uncle Buddy died."

"My Uncle Buddy is dead?"

"Yeah, the police came by and told granny, and now she's out taking care of the funeral arrangements."

"Why didn't you go?"

"Well, Mom, came over to talk. I saw her when I first got here and it didn't go too well but this time it was much better. She said that you called her. Are you two going to get back together?"

"Jewels, I don't know about that. We can talk about that later. Anything else happened that I should know about?"

"No, that's it."

"Did your grandmother tell you when the funeral was going to be?"

"No, she probably will when she comes back. How was your trip to Vegas?"

"It was nice. Have you packed everything for tomorrow?"

"No, not yet. I will do it before I go to bed."

"Well, tell your grandmother to call me when she gets in."

"Okay."

"I love you."

"I love you, too, Daddy."

I can't believe she thinks her mother and I are going to get back together. It's been a long time since Tracie and I have been together and my love for her has grown apart. I hope this is not going to make Jewels act differently toward Sade.

I can't believe my uncle is dead. Uncle Buddy was the family comedian. He used to love telling us dirty jokes. I remember when I caught him looking at a dirty magazine he looked at me and started laughing. He said, "Son, you will understand one of these days." And sure enough I did. I hid a stack of them under my mattress so my mother couldn't find them. Whenever I opened them up I think back to what he said and started laughing.

I hope my mom is handling this well. I wish she would have gotten the cell phone like I wanted her to then I would be able to call and get more information from her. Uncle Buddy was the last family member out there with my mother. Maybe now I can persuade her to move here with us. I know it's going to be hard but it's worth the try. I laid my head down and thought of all the things that had happened and hoped that everything would turn out as I planned.

I woke up the next day getting ready to pick up Jewels and I couldn't stop thinking about how I was going to tell her about Sade. I called my mother to see if Jewels and her friend were getting ready.

"Yes," she said. "Now, baby, your Uncle Buddy's funeral is going to be this weekend and I hope you will be able to make it."

"Momma, don't you think you should move to Dallas since there are no other family members out there?"

"Your mother is grown and I can take care of myself. I love it here and besides what will my bingo buddies do without me. I keep it *crunk*."

"You keep it what?" I asked.

"Crunk! I think I'm using it right."

"Momma, where did you get that from?"

"That's a new word I learned from Jewels and her friend."

"Okay, let's leave that word to the kids. You know that young lady I went to Vegas with?"

"Who? Sade?"

"Yeah."

"Oh, Sade is a nice girl. You should think about marrying her. She seems like good people."

"Funny you should say that, I asked her to marry me."

"You did, that's wonderful. Have you told Jewels?"

"No, I want to wait until she gets here before I tell here."

"I don't know. She might not take it too well. She was really hoping that you and Tracie would get back together."

"I could tell by the way she was talking about her last night. Tracie is not the one for me and Jewels will just have to understand."

"That's easier said than done. Good luck to you, Son, I think you made the right choice."

"Me, too, I will get a ticket for the funeral."

"Okay, baby, I will see you when you get here."

"I love you, Mother."

"I love you, too, baby."

When I got to the airport I went to baggage claims to wait for Jewels. The minute I walked in I could hear her say, "Daddy, Daddy, here I am." She ran into my arms and said, "I missed you, Daddy." I asked Natalie if she had a good time and she said, "Yes." We stopped to get something to eat and went home.

I called Jewels into the room and told her about Sade. She wasn't happy about it.

"I thought you and mother was going to get back together," she said.

"Your mother and I have grown apart and have moved on with our lives."

"How you can say that? Momma has changed for the better. I know we had some hard times but we can get through it. We just have to try."

"Jewels, I know that you are taking this hard but I hope that you will respect my decision."

"Have you spoken to mother? She told me that you called."

"I haven't had a chance to speak with your mother. I left her a message while I was in Vegas. I was so happy to hear that she had turned her life around and I wanted to talk to her about it."

"Why didn't you ask how I felt before you asked Sade to marry you?"

"I didn't think I had to. I'm your father and I would hate to think that you didn't trust my judgment."

"No, Daddy, it's not that. I just thought that since mother had gotten herself together things could go back to the way they were."

"Jewels, sometimes things look like they're going well but if you looked at the situation closely you will see that it's not. Your mother hurt me so bad and even though I forgave her, it really would be hard for me to trust her in that way. I don't think I would be able to handle that kind of pain from your mother again. I gave her my all and that's something men don't do very often. If I were to go back she wouldn't have my all and I don't want to waste her time or mine."

"Are you sure that there is no way? Just talk to her, we can make this work if we try. She looks so different and she has this glow about her that I never seen before."

"I just want you to focus on having a closer relationship with her. Don't waste your time worrying about what Tracie and I are going to do."

"Okay, Daddy."

I could tell that she wasn't happy with the idea of her mother and me not getting back together but I just couldn't see the logic in that. What Tracie and I had was fun while it lasted and now I see myself going in a different direction. I wish the best for her and now that she's gotten herself together I know she will have a good life. Now Jewels can have the relationship that she always wanted with her mother. And the time has come for me to have the type of relationship that I always wanted with a woman.

Engagement

Sade

He did it. I'm getting married. I thought it would never happen. I hope Jewels and I will hit it off. I've heard some good and bad stories about stepkids. I hope nothing but the best come this way. I can't wait until I tell my best friend Paige. She thought she would be the first one to get married but I'm going to prove her wrong.

If everything goes well we can be married in six months. What colors should I choose? How many bridesmaids do I want? I know Paige already has given herself the maid of honor title. She will be so upset if I don't pick her.

I don't know why I'm trying to hide the fear that I have in my heart about my relationship with Jewels. I always wanted to get married but I never thought it would come with an already-made family. Kids these days are full of attitude and they know how to get their way. I heard a daughter's bond with her father is something that no one can separate. I remember a story that my friend girl told me. She was telling me how her stepdaughter used to come home with an attitude and her husband would always run to her rescue. There were times when he thought she was jealous of his daughter. She couldn't understand how a grown woman would be jealous of a child but she guess there must be some woman out there he has come across who is like that.

I can't see myself being that woman but who knows, I could be. I've never been in that situation before so I really can't say how I would react. She could be the rebellious type who does the opposite just to get her father's attention. She could even make up stories about me that could make her father doubt my credibility. Who knows, she may try to make my life miserable so I wouldn't want to stay, so she will have him all to herself.

Am I really, ready for something like this? Being a stepmother seems to be more work than being a wife. What if her mother tries to turn her against me by feeding her negative things about me, and blaming me for her and Mike not being together? I have a funny feeling that she's going to come head on with attitude especially if she thinks her parents have a chance of getting back together. I've seen it many of times on the talk shows.

What if I made the wrong decision when I said yes to his proposal? I didn't think it would be this hard. I must have made the right decision because it feels right. I know marriage isn't going to be easy. Many couples have told me that it's a lot of work. I've been Miss Independent for all these years, being able to leave when I want to and spend as much as I want to. It's been just me, and now I have to think about two other people. Does he even want any more kids? There are so many things that I didn't think about before I said yes. Maybe it was just the sex that made me want him. What am I doing to myself? He is the one, I know he is.

I'm going to think positive. I think we could become real good friends. Oh how I hope this is true. I can't let her stand in the way of our love. Listen to you, Sade, you're talking about a child. I think I'm going to wait before I tell anyone just in case Jewels doesn't accept it. All I can do is wait on his call, and that's something that I'm not good at doing, but I'm trying.

I'm still shocked that he actually did it. I didn't think he would especially after he was tripping when we were in Vegas. He asked me if we could dance and of course I said, "Sure." So while we were dancing he looked at me and said, "You are a very special person and you possess so much beauty inside. When I'm around you I get a sense of peace." I had this funny look on my face wondering where all this was coming from and then he reached into his pocket and took out a ring. My eyes started tearing up. I was so shocked. He grabbed my left hand and while he was putting the ring on my finger he said, "Because of that, I want you to be with me for the rest of my life. Will you marry me?" I just stood there staring at that diamond. Then he said, "Well, will you?" I looked him in his eyes and said, "Yes."

We began to kiss and that kiss felt different from all the other times we have ever kissed. It was like we were exchanging energy from one body to another just by us embracing one another. As we continued dancing my heart kept beating fast from excitement. After the song ended he looked me in my eyes and said, "Sade, I love you." At that moment, my knees started to feel weak. I couldn't take it anymore. My body had too much excitement for one night. I whispered, "I love you too," into his ear and laid in his arms. We cuddled all night and before I knew it, I was asleep. I didn't think the trip was going to end that way but I'm glad it did.

Today Jewels is due to be back in town. I couldn't think straight. I was waiting on Mike's call to tell me how she took it but he never did. I wanted to call him so bad but I thought that if I did I might interrupt his conversation with Jewels. I have a funny feeling about this. I called my friend Paige to see how she was doing and to take my mind off of it. She started telling me about her boyfriend and how she caught him cheating. I don't understand why this girl always pick men who are not worthy of her time. I think she finds them a challenge and someone she can mold to her liking. It hasn't worked yet so I really don't understand why she is still trying. She told me she came home early one day from work and noticed an unfamiliar car parked on the side of the house. She didn't want to make a noise by going through the garage so she decided to park her car on the opposite side just in case they looked out the window. She went through the front door and up the stairs. As she got to the middle step she started hearing noises. She then began to take her belt off and continue to go up the remaining steps. When she opened the door anger sat in and before she knew it she ran up to her ex and began hitting him with her belt. As he jumped up she was able to see the other woman.

When the woman turned around she realized that it wasn't a woman, but a man. At that moment, she began beating him and calling them all kinds of names. My eyes bucked out and my mouth dropped. Seeing my man with another man is something that I don't want to experience.

She kept telling me how she beat them right out of her house. I asked her if she had talked to him since then and she said no. She said that he kept calling trying to explain by telling her that it wasn't what she thought it was and that he's not gay. He had the nerve to tell her that if she had let him do it to her he wouldn't have had to turn to a man. I couldn't believe my ears. How could he even try to turn that one around?

"So what are you going to do?" I asked.

"I don't know. I wish he would stop calling me. I get sick just thinking about it. I just don't understand it. Why me? Why do I keep attracting no-good men?"

"Well, Paige, you have to think about how you're coming across to them. Examine yourself."

"What are you trying to say, Sade?"

"All I'm saying is, well uh, how I can put this…"

"Just say it."

"It's something about the way you carry yourself and the places that you go that attracts the people that you date. I mean you settle a lot. You come off kind of desperate. You don't have any type of standards, it's like if they have a penis then you're in."

"It sounds like you're calling me a whore in a nice way."

"I'm not calling you a whore, well, since you said it I guess it can be looked at that way."

"I can't believe my best friend just called me a whore."

"Technically I didn't call you that you put it out there. Paige, for the past three years you've been dating busters. Remember Big T the one with no job but a dream. Always saying that he's going to do this and that but it never manifested. And what about JT, the two-bit hustler who wasn't bringing in enough money to pay your four-hundred-dollar car note, that you were letting him drive around in. And what about—"

"Okay, I get the picture."

"Paige, not only that, but you've never given yourself time to get rid of anyone of them. One week after Big T you meet JT. A break up is just like a bad cold it takes time to get over it and if you get out to soon it can spread to others. You have to take some time away from it all to clear your mind and release yourself from that person before jumping into another relationship."

"Yeah, you're right."

"Think of it this way, you have a week's worth of dirty laundry in a basket waiting to be washed. The next week you put more clothes in the basket. After a while if you don't wash those clothes they will begin to smell up the place. You might get permanent stains on some of the clothes because you let them sit too long. That's how our body, mind, and spirits are. We need to take some time away from it all and cleanse ourselves. Right now, Paige, you have about five years' worth of dirt in you because you haven't taken the time out to clean up."

"I feel you. Why did you wait so long to tell me this?"

"I've been telling you this but you just didn't listen. Sometimes we have to go through some things to get where God wants us to be."

"There you go with that God stuff."

"You might want to try Him. You've tried everything else and look what it has gotten you."

"You know what, you're right about that. I don't know, I'll think about it. Let me go, listening to that laundry story reminded me about the clothes that I need to be washing. I will call you later."

"Okay," I said and we hung up the phone. Wow, that girl's life gets more interesting by the minute. Hopefully my words will encourage her to start thinking about God more.

I laid on the couch waiting on the phone call from Mike so I could find out how Jewels felt about the whole thing. I know that God has a plan and he will work it out for the good.

Out of Control

Jewels

I can't believe he's going to marry that lady. She doesn't even seem like his type. Why can't everything go back to the way it was? I know he said he and my mom's relationship wasn't all that good but I know if they work at it things can get better. I can't worry myself about that since it's out of my control or maybe it isn't. I can make her life a living hell without my dad even recognizing it. She will hate the fact that she said "I Do" when I'm finished with her.

Natalie's mother had left her a couple of messages while we were gone. She told Natalie that she was sorry and that she wants her to come back home. Natalie was so surprised and she was happy. She couldn't believe that her mother really wants her to come back home. "I guess the conversation with your daddy helped a lot," Natalie said.

"Yeah, he told me that she listened and she didn't get loud or upset."

"Really, I wish I could have been on three-way when that call was made. I've never heard her talk calm to anyone that was trying to tell her that she was in the wrong."

"My daddy says things in a way that is not attacking. It's real weird. I've heard him do it with my mom."

"I'm glad that she wants me back but I'm wondering if things will change. I miss my brothers and sisters but I don't want to go back if she's going to continue to treat me the way that she does."

"Well you will never know unless you go back. I've enjoyed your company but I know that you're going to go through things that only a mother would be able to direct you. That's why I'm kind of glad that I was able to talk to my mother because I know I'm going to need her."

"What about your father's friend? She's real cool. She could probably help you with things."

"She's not my mother and I don't want her help. She just wants my daddy."

"How can you say that? She's already guilty in your eyes and she hasn't done anything yet. What if your mother never called or wanted to see you? You talk to me about God and you pray every night before you go to bed and look how you act. Maybe God has brought her into your life for a reason. Don't cast her out yet, your pride is going to make you miss out on something."

"I don't know. You might be right. Maybe I will ask my daddy if she could stay here with me while he goes to the funeral. That will give us some one on one time together. Then I can see what she's really about."

"You think he would? You don't want to go to your uncle Buddy's funeral?"

"I never met him. I've already spent time with my granny so why waste the money. He wants us to get to know each other anyway, and if I go to him with this it will look like I'm trying."

"Just make sure you have good intentions."

"I do, like you said I'm judging her before giving her a chance to prove herself. She might just be the best thing that has happened to my father and me."

"Okay, well I guess I will go home. I really want to hang out with my family."

"I will let my dad know so he can drop you off."

"Okay, thanks, Jewels, for everything. I probably wouldn't have ever experienced what I did if it wasn't for you."

"No problem, that's what friends are for."

I wonder if Natalie is right about my intentions and giving Sade a chance. I walked in my dad's room to tell him that Natalie was ready to go home.

"I guess your talk with her mother really worked."

"Oh really, what did she say?" he asked.

"Well, she left her a message wanting her to come back home and now she's packing."

"Well, that's wonderful. I'm glad that she's going back to her family. There's nothing like being with your folks."

"See, Daddy, you said it. There is nothing like being with your family, so why can't we be a family again?"

He looked at me and said, "Jewels, stop it. This is how it's going to be. Don't try to force something that's never going to happen."

The look on his face scared me. I knew right then he meant business. My daddy never really gets upset and when he does you better step back.

I said, "Okay," and walked out of his room. I told Natalie that my dad would be ready to take her home in a minute. I forgot to mention staying here with Sade while he goes to the funeral. I will save that for the conversation on our way back from dropping Natalie off at home.

While we waited on my dad I got on the computer to check my e-mails. My grandmother lives like she's in the country, she doesn't have cable, DSL, or anything. I was having withdrawals from not chatting online with my friends. The inbox pulled up and showed that I had fifty e-mails. A lot of them were junk mails. I noticed one that had "I'm sorry" in the subject line. I opened it up and it was from Troy. I couldn't believe it, after almost two years he pops up. How did he get my e-mail address anyway? I started reading the letter and it says,

Jewels,

It's been a long time since we've spoken and for some strange reason I've been thinking about you. I feel so bad about how I did you. I really was starting to like you but when your mother called she started telling me things about you that made me look at you differently. For one, I didn't know that you were twelve years old when we started talking. I felt betrayed. I was really starting to trust you. Your mother asked me what happened and I didn't want to tell her at first but she told me if I didn't she will call the police on me. So I did. She asked me how it was. That was kind of weird to me but out of fear I told her that you were all right for a virgin and then she told me that you wasn't one. After that I decided not to call you anymore because I thought you were pretending to be someone you were not. The other day when I was in Bible study the preacher asked if there were people in your life that you think that you've hurt and your name came across my mind. I had your old e-mail address from when we used to talk so I decided to write hoping that it will go through. I'm really, really sorry about the way I left and the things I said. I hope you accept my apologies and I would love to hear from you. We moved to Dallas a few months ago so I know I won't be able to see you but we can talk via e-mail if you like.

Yours truly,
Troy

I can't believe it. Troy really liked me. I could get mad at my mother but why, that was the past and we're starting over. I wonder if I should e-mail him back and let him know that I now live in Dallas. I'm going to wait before I respond. I need to let it all soak in.

"Jewels, I'm ready." My dad said.

"Okay we're coming down." I looked at Natalie. "Are you ready?" I asked.

"Yeah, I really think it's time," she said. We got in the car and began to drive down the highway. I kept thinking about Troy and his e-mail. It's a relief to know that he really thought I was special and that he would have continued to hang out with me if my mother wouldn't have butted in. I wonder if I should believe my mother or him, their versions are so different. *You know it really doesn't matter*, I thought. They both apologized and that's what counts.

When we got to her house Natalie looked kind of scared but when her little sister ran out the door her face lit up. She didn't let her get out the car good, she wanted hugs and kisses from Natalie. Natalie picked her up and hugged her so tight, tears started fallen down Natalie's face. She was happy to be home. Her mother came out the door. She had her daisy dukes on with this sports bra that she was wearing as a shirt. She had a red ponytail going down her back and a ring on every finger. She walked to the window and said, "Hello." She had a gold tooth in the front with sexy carved in it.

My dad looked at her and said, "Hello."

"Well, I want to thank you for looking after my daughter and also for the phone call."

"You're welcome," he said.

"You helped me see some things about myself that I didn't know that I had inside. I'm trying to work on them."

"If you believe that you can change then a change will happen."

"Please keep me in your prayers. I thank you dearly for the clothes that you bought and the trip to LA. I know she had a good time.

"She did," I said.

"I don't want to hold you two long and thank you again for all that you have done

My dad said, "You're welcome," and drove off.

My dad had a smile on his face. I knew he had some funny thoughts running through his head.

"What are you thinking about?" I asked.

"Oh nothing, she just reminds me a little bit of your mother. That's how your mother would have turned out if she hadn't gone off to college. I'm not saying that's a bad thing but it's a place of entrapment. Most people that live that way are not motivated to move up and it's probably because they don't think they have the tools to do it. I just thank God that I was motivated to want more and do more. At times I wanted to be lazy but I didn't let lazy take over me."

"Will she always be at that level?"

"It only depends on her drive. If you don't possess that drive inside of you, you will always be stuck in the driveway."

"I don't want to be stuck in the driveway," I said.

"Well only you can stop that from happening."

"I don't mean to get off the subject, Daddy, but I was thinking that I could stay here while you go to the funeral. I mean I just left LA and it doesn't make sense for you to spend money on another ticket."

"When have you ever been worried about money? You're the queen of spending. I know you don't think I'm going to let you stay here by yourself."

"No, Daddy, I wanted Sade to stay here with me. I know that she's someone special in your life and I just thought it would be a good idea for us to get to know each other one on one."

"What are you up to, Angel?"

"Nothing. You made it loud and clear that you and mother don't have a chance of getting back together. So, I might as well accept that fact and make the best of the situation."

"I'm so proud of you."

I looked out the window as he drove down the highway wondering if hanging with Sade for a whole weekend is something that I really wanted to do.

Accident

Mike

Sade was happy to hear that Jewels wanted her to stay with her while I was out of town. When I got to my mom's house in LA, all I could do was smile. Everything is still the same. The two-story white house with the rocking swing on the porch. I remember my mother and me sitting outside on the swing while she read me a story. She ran out the house with a smile saying, "My Baby." It's seems like it's been forever since I've seen you. She hit my shoulder and said, "Don't let it be this long before I see you again." We walked in the house and sat on the couch. She started telling me how much she enjoyed Jewels and her friend's company. She had forgotten how it was having kids around the house.

"They taught me a new word every day. They were so cute. Does Tracie know that you're out here?" she asked.

"No, but I want to talk to her before I leave."

"Yeah, I think that would be a good idea. She came over the other night and brought me some food."

"Food, did she cook it?"

"Yeah I think so, it was really good too. So did you tell Jewels about Sade?"

"Yes, she was all upset at first and then she changed. She wanted Sade to stay with her at the house while I came out here."

"I hope she isn't up to anything. You know she has her mother in her."

"I know. I asked her what she was up to and she said nothing."

"I know you didn't think she would actually tell you, did you?"

"Well, if she has bad intentions they will soon come out."

"The wake went okay. You know, I didn't realize how many young ladies knew Buddy. It was one girl who looked like she was in her thirties. She started screaming, "Get up, Buddy, get up," and then she began to shake him and before we knew it she was in the casket with him. The security men ran to the casket and pulled her out. I couldn't believe it. I had one lady come over here trying to see if Buddy's will mentioned anything about a son. I looked at her and said, "Baby, the only money Buddy had was in his pocket and you might want to check the lady from the wake to see if she had gotten him for it." I started laughing.

"Did Uncle Buddy have a will?"

"Yeah, he had one. I was surprised to hear that he left it all to me. It was about two hundred thousand dollars."

"Two hundred thousand, what are you going to do with all that?"

"Well, I'm going to put up a college fund for Jewels and then I was thinking about getting a makeover to this house. It's been this way since you were a baby. It's time for me to modernize the place. Oh I almost forgot, me and one of my bingo friends are thinking about going on a cruise."

"You've thought this through haven't you, Momma? Did Buddy have any kids?"

"Baby, I don't know. I didn't know he had so many young ladies in his life."

"What if he really has a son?"

"Well, I will have to see proof. I ended up telling the lady to get proof and once she provides that I will give the child something. Let me go into this kitchen and fix you something to eat. I know you have to be hungry. Does Sade know how to cook? You can't be marrying someone who can't feed you right."

"She's proven herself in that area, even Jewels said she could. Well, Momma, I'm going to go take a shower and I will come down when I'm finished."

"Okay, baby."

As I'm walking up the stairs my cell phone rings and it's Jewels asking me how everything was going. "Fine," I said.

"Is grandmother doing okay?"

"Yes she is. She's downstairs cooking now. How is it going with you and Sade?"

"It's fine we're on our way to the movies."

"Cool, don't do anything crazy, Jewels."

"I won't, Daddy."

"Okay, baby, Daddy, loves you."

"I love you, too."

Sometimes I wonder if she forgets that I'm the parent. When I got out of the shower I smelled my mother's fried chicken. As I started down the stairs I heard laughter. When I got to the end of the steps I turned toward the kitchen and there she was my ex-wife. Jewels wasn't lying she does have this glow about her. She ran up to me and gave me a hug and a kiss on the cheek.

"Nice to see you," I said.

"Nice to see you, too."

"So what are you doing around these parts?"

"I came by to see your mother."

"That's cool. Do you want to have something to eat?"

"No, I'm fine but I do want to talk to you for a minute."

"Let me eat something and we can take a walk."

"No need to take a walk. Me and some of my bingo friends are going out. They want to take me out so I won't have to think about Buddy," Mother said.

"Where are they taking you?" I asked.

"Out, see that's one reason why I don't want to move down there with you. I can see right now you'll be all in my business."

"Tell him, Momma," Tracie said.

"Okay, well you go on and have some fun. Try not to be out so late," I said.

She turned around and said, "I'm grown, Son," and walked out of the front door.

"Your mother is still crazy," Tracie said as we sat on the love seat in the living room.

"I know."

"So how has life been treating you since we've separated?" she asked.

"It was rough at first but it seems like everything is falling into place."

"That's good to hear. I really want to apologize for all I did while we were married."

"Tracie, we both had our faults. I was working all the time and not giving you the time you needed. I didn't cater to your needs and that cost me."

"Yeah but you were out there trying to make a living for us. I should have taken that into consideration. I mean if there were needs that I wasn't getting from you I should have communicated that to you. A lot of marriages break up because of lack of communication."

"I can agree we didn't communicate like we should have. If I did anything to hurt you within our marriage, I want to apologize. I mean I'm not going to sit here and act like I was the perfect husband because if I was we would still be together."

"You were almost perfect. You gave me everything that I wanted."

"Yeah but I didn't give you everything that you needed."

She started rubbing my face, my mind went back, and before I knew it, we were kissing. I picked her up and carried her up the stairs. As we were having sex I started feeling guilty but I couldn't get her off of me. I opened my eyes and I saw Sade, I closed them real fast and opened them back up and it was Tracie. My mind was going crazy. This wasn't in the plan. I have to get her off of me, but it feels so good. Oh, Lord, I don't have a condom on. What was I thinking being left alone with this woman? She started moaning and then she screamed, "Oh Mark."

Who is Mark? I thought. Mark must be her man. If she had a man why did she started touching on me. This is crazy. "Get up," I said as I started pushing her off of me but she didn't budge. I said it again, but it was too late. She jumped up and I looked at her and asked, "What have we done?"

"I don't know, it all happened so fast."

"Who's Mark?"

"Mark?" she asked. "Where did that name come from?"

"That was the name you were screaming when you were on top of me."

"Oh I'm so sorry. Mark is the new man in my life. I don't know why his name came out, that's weird."

"No, what we just did was weird. This must stay between you and me. I'm engaged to be married and she can't find out about this."

"Jewels didn't tell me that you were engaged."

"She didn't know at the time. I told her when she got back home."

"Wow, what happened in this room stays in this room."

Why me, why can't I control the man in my pants? We started putting on our clothes. "So I guess this is it?" she asked.

"I guess so."

"I thought we said 'forever.'"

"We were young then and in the midst of our marriage I realize nothing is forever."

"I still hold a part of you in my heart. When I got your phone call I really thought there was a chance for the two of us to get back together. Wow, we really grew apart."

"When we got back together in college I think we took for granted the knowledge that we had about each other. Things had happened in both of our lives and we didn't fill each other in. We took for granted that everything was still the same as it was when I left. You didn't tell me about the guy whom you started going with after I left and the things he made you do. That stuff can mess a person up on the inside and then you brought that to me hoping that I was your cure. You expected me to heal you without telling me what was wrong with you. Tracie, you were my first love and I will always cherish our relationship. I will continue to push the communication with you and Jewels because I feel that little girls need their mother. Now that she's a teenager there are going to be some things that she will go through only a woman would understand. I've talked to Sade about Jewels and she told me that she's not trying to take your place. She wants to be here to help in every way that she can."

"I was wrong for not being completely honest about the lifestyle that I had before getting back with you. I'm glad to hear that you've found you someone else. I guess this is it. Like I said before what happened in this room will stay in the room."

As she walked out of the door, I watched her get into her car. Guilt began to sit in. I couldn't believe I cheated on Sade, of all women, why her. I went back upstairs and took another shower. I changed the sheets on the guest bed and put them in the washer. I put some new ones on because I didn't want any type of evidence of sex when my mom came.

I laid down in the bed and closed my eyes and before I knew it my mother was telling me that breakfast was ready. I got up and went into the bathroom to wash my face and brush my teeth. I still couldn't stop thinking about last night. I don't know why I thought I could sleep the guilt away. I went downstairs and all I could smell were pancakes and eggs. My mother knows how to cook some home-made pancakes. They look so thick and fluffy on that plate and the eggs look so perfect. I sat down, said my grace, and began to eat. All I could do was moan. My stomach loves my mommas cooking. She pours me a glass of orange juice and sits down at the table. "You slept with her, didn't you?" she asked. I started choking off the food that was in my mouth.

"What did you say?" I asked.

"You slept with Tracie."

"What would make you say a thing like that?"

"The only time you wash sheets is to hide something. I found that out a long time ago when you and Tracie were living here. How are you going to explain that to Sade?"

"I wasn't going to say anything."

"Son, whatever you do don't go into another marriage with secrets especially secrets that could come back and haunt you."

"She might not want to marry me if I told her. And besides Tracie and I both agreed that what happened in that room will stay in that room."

"Haven't you learned anything yet? I bet Tracie said the same thing about the life she had before she got back with you. And you see how quickly it came out. Did you use protection?"

"Momma, I don't want to talk about my sex life with you."

"Well don't call me trying to see what you should do when you find out she's pregnant."

"What are you talking about? She's not pregnant."

"Oh so I guess you used a condom."

"I'm not saying that but I know she's not pregnant."

"If I were you I will tell Sade about this now before it comes back and bite you. Didn't I tell you to keep your legs closed? You have to learn how to control yourself."

"You're right, I don't know how I'm going to tell her but I will."

"Well you need to hurry up and get ready for the funeral. Buddy will be real mad if we're late. Don't you know that man wants us to play *Another One Bites the Dust*? I can't do that. People will look at me crazy."

"You have to grant him his wish. *Another One Bites the Dust*, that Uncle Buddy is crazy, you can't blame him for keeping it real."

I called Tracie before we left and told her that I've decided to go ahead and tell my fiancé what happened. She kept telling me how that wouldn't be a good idea and that she wouldn't want to marry me after she found out. If she doesn't then she wasn't the one in the first place. I hung up the phone and I prayed.

Momma broke down and allowed them to play *Another One Bites the Dust* as they were carrying Buddy to the car. I saw that lady momma was telling me about. She wanted to ride in the car with the casket. The security men had to grab her and pull her off of him. Mother grabbed my arm and said I'm going to see if she's going to fall in the hole with him once they start railing him down in the ground. I tried my best to hold my laugh in but I couldn't. I burst out laughing and everyone turned around and gave me this funny look. I was so embarrassed. We didn't see the lady at the gravesite. I guess she couldn't fathom seeing him going into the ground.

A lot of people came to mother's house after the funeral. I saw old cousins that I haven't seen in a long time. Food was everywhere. We had so much I didn't know where to start. I sat outside with my cousins and laughed about old times. It's sad that a death is what brought us all together. I guess everybody is so busy living his or her day-to-day life that before you know it time has passed and you haven't spoken to anyone. Needless to say, we exchanged numbers in hopes that we will continue to keep in touch.

Tracie didn't come over and I was kind of glad. Seeing her again this soon would have been very awkward. After everyone left I laid on the couch and started watching TV. Mother took everything well, I guess she did her mourning before I got here.

I slept hard last night. Mother fixed me breakfast and packed a lot of that leftover meat for me to take back to Dallas. She even put it in a carryout container. I started laughing.

"Ain't no sense all this food going to waste," she said.

I shook my head and smile. She gave me a hug and kissed me on my forehead.

"Now you start this relationship off right by telling the truth. You don't want to give Satan a reason to keep replaying the incident in your head."

"I will, Mother, I know it's the right thing to do."

The flight was quicker than normal it seemed. I drove up and there was my Angel outside in the dark on the porch talking on the phone. She got off and ran to the car.

"Hey, Daddy, how was your trip? Did you talk to mother? Didn't she look so beautiful?"

"Hold up, Angel, let me get out of the car first. I'm excited to see you, too. Yes, I saw your mother and yes she looked beautiful, but, Jewels, we're not getting back together so give it a rest."

I walked in and gave Sade a hug and a kiss.

"I missed you," she said.

"I missed you, too. How did everything go her with Jewels?"

"I think it went well, we went to the mall and to the movies. We really didn't talk much about one another. We were just enjoying each other's company. How was it there in LA?"

"It was fine. Can you believe my uncle Buddy requested *Another One Bites the Dust*?"

"You're playing, right?"

"Nope, Ma was so mad but she did it anyway."

"What's up, Mike? It seems like something is bothering you?"

I grabbed her and took her into the room. "I talked to Tracie while I was out there."

"Okay and."

"We ended up having sex."

"Excuse me, you did what?"

"I don't know how it happened, one minute we were talking and the next minute we were naked."

"I can't believe this, you went to LA for a funeral, and you ended up having sex with your ex-wife. Mike, what did I do to deserve this?"

"It was an accident. No meaning behind it whatsoever."

"It was an accident. What in the hell does that supposed to do for me? Still to this day, I can't understand how you can accidentally have sex with somebody. At some point you should have known that something was not right, especially if you have someone back home that you love and respect. I guess that's something you don't have with me. One day you're asking me to marry you and a few days later you're having sex with your ex. Did you use protection?"

"It happened so fast."

"I guess that means no. So you could be carrying some type of disease right now and don't even know it. She could be carrying your next baby at this moment and don't even know it. I can't look at you right now. I have to go."

"Wait, Sade, please don't leave like this. It's late and I don't want you to be driving on the road mad."

"Why in the hell are you worrying about me now? You weren't thinking too much about me when you were lying up with your ex."

"It wasn't like that, Sade, please believe me. I could have kept this from you but I didn't."

"Oh you're proud that you came forward. I must admit that was real manly of you. I will give you that but that still doesn't take away the hurt that I'm feeling right now."

Jewels walks in, "Is everything okay?" she asked.

"Yes," I said. "Now go to your room, Sade and I are talking."

She walks out and I pulled Sade back into my room and close the door.

"Look, Sade I know that you are mad and you have every right to be. If you don't want to marry me after this, I will respect your decision. I was wrong and I hated myself after the fact. I can't turn back the hands of time because if I could I would. Please stay here until in the morning. I really don't want you to drive while you're upset. You can have the bedroom and I will sleep in the guest room."

"No, I'm the guest in this house. I will sleep there."

She gets her things and leaves the room. What have I done? Maybe telling her wasn't the right thing to do. I should have kept it to myself as I planned on doing at first. I hope my momma was right about this.

He's Back

Jewels

I wonder what that was all about. I guess she won't last long. I didn't have to do anything after all. Too bad, I was starting to like her. I mean she seemed like she could be good people. I know my dad will tell me what happened. I'll just wait to see what he says. I can hear her crying. She sounds like she's in a lot of pain. I hate to see people hurting like that. I wonder if she needs someone to talk to. I should go down there. No, I better stay out of grown folks' business. What if he told her that he's still in love with my mother and they are getting back together, that would be cool. I knew, once he saw her he would fall right back in love. Now things can be like they used to be. Everything is turning out the way I wanted it to.

Oh well let me get off of that. I still can't believe Troy wants to hang out. I'm not for sure if I should do it though. He really did me wrong and it took me a while before I got over him. I really loved that boy. I know my dad always say that I'm too young to know what love is but I don't think so. What if I go back and things are not the same or what if going back to him would only bring back bad memories?

I don't know what to do. Maybe he is my true love. Why else would he try to get back in touch with me? I think I'm going to call him. It won't hurt to see how he's been doing. What if he wants to see me? Am I ready for that? My hands start to shake as I began dialing his number. I was hoping that he wouldn't answer that way I could leave a message and he would have to call me back. One ring, two rings, three rings, one more ring, and straight to voice mail. "Hello,"

Troy said. I couldn't say anything. I don't know what happened to my voice. "Hello," he said again.

"Hey."

"Hey, who is this?"

"This is Jewels."

"Hey, Jewels, I didn't think you were going to call."

"I still can't believe I did."

"I see you're calling from a Dallas number, are you down here?"

"Yeah, I live down here now. I thought I was getting away from my past but it seems like a part of it followed me."

"You sure it's not the other way around?"

"I'm sure."

"Maybe we could go out to eat or something."

"I don't know about that. I mean what if you haven't changed. Maybe you still that person that left me feeling like trash. It took me a long time to get over you."

"Please forgive me. I've changed and I know I was wrong. If I could turn back the hands of time and do things different I would, but I can't. Can we at least be friends?"

"Let me think about it. I never thought I would see or hear from you again. And now that I'm hearing your voice I can't help but to think about how you treated me."

"I don't want your last thought of me to be full of pain. Will you please let me make it up to you?"

He really wants to makes things better, I thought. I wonder why.

"Troy, if you even think about hurting me again I will make sure you regret the day you sent me that e-mail," I said.

"Thank you so much, Jewels. I promise you won't regret this."

We hung up the phone and I sat there wondering if he was playing me again. This time I will be ready.

I woke up to the sounds of the birds chirping at my window. The sun was shining and the trees were blowing. It was a beautiful day. I went down to the guest room to see if Sade was still here, but the room was empty. The bed was made and the curtains were open. The sun shined through the room and it was nice. I went to the kitchen to see if anyone was there and as I was walking into the kitchen I saw my daddy sitting on the couch watching TV. I walked over to him thinking how I'm going to get the dirt on last night. I sat down and said, "Good morning."

He looked at me and said, "Good morning, Angel."

"So what was last night all about?"

"Nothing you have to worry about."

At that moment I knew that he wasn't talking. I couldn't stop there. So I asked him if Sade was gone and this time he kept looking at the television and he said, "Yes, she's gone home." I'm not going to get anything out of him about what happened on last night so I asked him what he was doing today and he said he didn't know. I could tell that he really didn't want to be bothered with so I went into the kitchen, fixed me a bowl of cereal, and went back to my room.

I called Natalie to see if she was doing anything and she didn't answer. *What now?* I thought. My dad was in the dumps, my best friend is gone, and I don't have anything to do. I picked the phone and called Troy. Why am I doing this to myself? He picks up. "Hey, Troy," I said.

"Hey, Jewels, I didn't think you were going to call me anymore based on the conversation we had last night. I know you said that you would give me another chance but to be honest I really didn't believe you."

"Well, I guess you were wrong in not believing me, so do you want to meet me at the park or what?" I asked.

"Sure."

I told him where the park was by my house and he said that he would meet me there in thirty minutes. I started getting dressed and my dad walked in and asked me where I was getting ready to go. *Should I lie?* I thought. "To the park," I said. "I didn't think you wanted to be bothered so I'm just going to walk up there and hang out for a while."

"What do you call 'a while'?"

"Oh I don't know maybe about thirty minutes to an hour."

"Are you meeting someone out there?"

Why is he giving me the third degree? Should I tell him that I spoke with Troy and that he was meeting me out there? No, I better not. I know if I do he's not going to let me go. I think I better because I know he will find out somehow and my life wouldn't be right once he did. "An old friend," I said hoping that he wouldn't ask any more questions.

"Is this old friend a male or a female?"

I knew it. Why did he have to ask that question? What should I say, think Jewels. Before I knew it, the words "female" came out of my mouth. I can't believe I just lied to my daddy. I wonder if he really believes it. He gave me this funny look and said, "Have fun," and walked out of my room. I hope that lie was worth it. I hope he doesn't find out.

As I was walking down to the park all I could do was think about how much my life has changed since I've left LA. And I was happy, my mind was so confused during one stage of my life and now my mind is much clearer.

When I arrived at the park there were a lot of people there but no Troy. I didn't realize that people be out and about so early in the morning. I guess eleven is not too earlier. I started getting butterflies wondering whether he was going to show up or not. I hope he still looks good like he did when I met him a few years ago.

Thirty minutes has passed and Troy is not here. My butterflies started to turn into anger and disbelief. I couldn't believe that I fell for him again. I got up to leave and when I turned around there he was standing there looking so fine. In one hand he had a dozen of roses and in his other hand he had a bag from McDonald's that had pancakes, eggs, and orange juice in it.

"What took you so long?" I asked.

"Well, I didn't realize how long it was going to take me to make the stops that I needed to make. I hope you're not mad at me," he said.

"These flowers are making it real hard for me to get upset," I answered.

"Jewels, you still look as beautiful as you did the day I met you."

"Oh really."

"I really hate that we didn't stay together. I don't know what I was thinking back then."

"So what made you think of me after all these years?" I asked.

"Well, my mom's job transferred her to Dallas about a year ago. While I was unpacking I found a picture of you and me along with a letter that you wrote. That made me think about our relationship and the bad things that I did to you. Then when I went to church the preacher just confirmed how wrong I was. It took me a while before I wrote the e-mail that I sent you."

"I'm glad that you sent me the e-mail. I didn't think you had a heart. I really haven't been able to trust anybody. You were my first true love. I thought we were going to last forever. I still can't believe how many nights I cried over you. Being with you right now is hard because a part of me still loves you. I don't understand why but I do."

"You might not believe me, Jewels, but a part of me still loves you. I tried dating other females after I stopped talking to you but they never made me laugh like you did. I didn't realize how much I really cared about you until you were gone."

"Why are you here now? What are you expecting to gain from this?"

"I really want us to start over if we could. I believe that we can make it."

"Troy, I don't know. I mean you're about to graduate and after that it's off to college. I don't see any future in that. I think we should just be friends."

"Jewels, I'm not going off to college, so you don't have to worry about that. I really think we could make this work. But if you just want to friends I will respect that."

"I think we should take it slow and be friends. If a relationship is supposed to come out of it then it will. I really enjoyed this time that we had and thank you again for the flowers and the breakfast. I think I better go before my dad starts calling me on my cell.

"It was nice seeing you again, Jewels, and I hope that this won't be the last time that we see each other. Do you want me to take you to your house?"

"That's okay, I can walk. I will call you tonight."

"Okay."

He gave me a hug and kissed me on my forehead. I walked down the street wondering if another relationship with him will work. I better take it slow because pain is not something that I'm ready to run back to.

Closure

Sade

"Paige, I can't believe that you are sitting here trying to talk me into going back with Mike. I mean he had sex with his ex. What makes you think he's not going to do it again?"

"Sade, the man didn't have to tell you. The fact that he did lets me know that he have much respect for you and want nothing but honesty to come out of the relationship, don't let that one night mess up your entire life."

"Yeah, you're right but what if it's not over. I mean what if he still has feelings for her and wants to get back with her?"

"Sade, are you listening to yourself? If the man still had feelings for the woman he would have told you that he slept with her, it was good, and they've decided that they should be together. Did he say that? No, he didn't. I would think of them having sex as their way of closing out the relationship. Girl, you know how it is when you want to get it just one more time. Now you can't tell me that you never done that."

"I must admit I have done that in my day."

"At least he did it before the wedding ceremony. You got to give him credit for that. If you think about it, it probably wasn't planned."

"That's what he said."

"Don't let that man go, girl."

"You're right. I'm going to call him after you leave."

"Well let me go I don't want to be the reason for you not getting back with your man."

"Whatever, Paige, I will talk to you later."

I walked her to the door and went in my room. I don't know what to do. I know that I really love this man and I feel in my bones that he is the one for me but how can I go back to him knowing that he has been with his ex. I understand what Paige was saying but part of me is still scared. I would hate to give my all to someone and my heart end up getting broken. What am I going to do? I can't stop thinking about this man. When I woke up the next morning from his house I felt so weird leaving. It was like I was leaving my home. I actually felt like I belong there. Jewels and I had a wonderful weekend. I finally felt as if we were connecting.

I wonder who this could be knocking at my door. "Who is it?" I asked.

"It's me, Mike."

What is he doing here? I have to open the door since he heard my voice. I opened the door and all I could see is this tall black chocolate man who I am totally in love with.

"Can I come in?"

"Yes."

Damn he looks good. He had the nerve to put on the shirt I like. I bet he's doing this on purpose trying to see if I will fall weak for him. Little did he know I felt weak the minute I opened the door and saw his beautiful black body.

"So, did I interrupt something?" he asked.

"No."

Then he grabbed me and started kissing my neck and whispering "I love you" into my ear. I'm melting right into his arms. I can feel myself sinking. He picks me up and takes me into the room. I don't have any strength in my body to fight and to be honest I really don't want to.

I woke up with him lying next to me. I can't do anything but stare at his fine sexy self. His dark skin is so smooth and soft. I can't let this man leave. The fact that he came here proves he doesn't want me to go anywhere either. I can give him another chance. I know if it was me I would want one. He turns over and looks at me and says, "Good morning, beautiful."

I smile and said, "Good morning to you, handsome. I forgive you for what you did with your ex. I just want you to promise me that it will never happen again. I would hate to walk down the aisle wondering if you will ever go down that road again."

"Baby, you don't have to worry about that. I have no plans to go down any other road but yours."

"Baby, what would you like to have for breakfast?" I asked.

"I got it this time, you tell me what you want," he asked.

"An omelet with turkey and cheese would be nice."

"I'm going to need your help with that," he said.

"No problem. I can do that."

We walked into the kitchen and began to fix breakfast. Everything felt normal. Being with him brings something out of me that I never knew I had. I don't know what I was thinking about. I can't let him get away from me.

After eating breakfast he left to go home to get ready for work. I had to call in. My body was like an emotional roller coaster and I need a day to myself to get my mind back together. I laid in bed for about an hour and then I got up, showered, and called Paige. I needed to go shopping and I know Paige is the girl to go with. It didn't take her long to get to the house. I couldn't get the word "shopping" out of my mouth and she was already knocking at my door.

"Dang, Paige, did you sleep in my backyard? How did you get here so fast?"

"I didn't sleep in your backyard but I did sleep in your next-door neighbor's bed."

"You mean Tyson? Please don't tell me you slept with Tyson."

"Okay, I won't then," she said.

"Paige, you better slow your nasty self down. Tyson don't want nothing but what's in the pants."

"That's cool, girl, because that's all I wanted."

"Paige, I really think you need some help. You got some type of disease."

"I don't have a disease, don't put that on me."

"I won't be the one putting it on you. I keep telling you, girl, you better slow down before something catch up and bite you."

"Did you call me over here to go shopping or to talk about my sex life?"

"I called you over here to shop. Are you ready?"

"You know I was born ready. Shopping is my first, middle, and last name."

We jumped in the car and she asked me what Mike was doing over here. "What do you mean what was he doing over here?" I asked.

"I noticed that he came over last night and the car didn't leave until this morning."

"You had enough time to look out of the window while you were taking care of business."

"Hey, you know how I do it."

"Since you must know Mike and I have gotten back together."

"He put it on you, didn't he? I know he did. He made you remember why you fell for him in the first place. I bet you didn't think about ole girl at all."

"Whatever, no I didn't think about her. I took your advice and him coming over just helped me make the final decision. I really care for that man and I would be a crazy person if I let him go."

"I'm so glad that you found happiness. I can see the glow on your face. I want that. I know I might come across all wild and crazy but all I'm trying to do is find someone who can give me what you got."

"Paige, how do you expect to find real love if you keep giving yourself away to all these different men? I mean no man is going to want a woman who doesn't love herself enough to wait on him."

"I don't know how to be any other way. I look at you Sade and you're beautiful, you have a good job, a nice crib, and now a good man by your side. And what do I have, nothing. I can barely pay my rent. I can't find a good job because I never completed high school. Everywhere I go they ask to see my high school diploma."

"Paige, why didn't you tell me this, I'm a CEO I can create you a job?"

"I didn't want to have to come to you for money. I wanted you to think that I was on the same level as you."

"Same level, what is that supposed to mean? We are best friends. There are things that I don't know that you will be able to help me on and vice versa. We are not going to be alike because we are two different people. Just because you don't make the same amount of money that I make doesn't mean that we are not on the same level. I want you at my job first thing tomorrow. I will find some work for you to do. I see we have to build up your self-esteem because a real man is not going to want a woman who doesn't love herself or think that she's worth loving."

"Thanks, Sade. You really don't have to do this and I appreciate you for what you are doing. I love you, girl, and that's coming straight from the heart."

"I love you, too."

We did our shopping thing and we went home. I couldn't believe that the friend that I always knew didn't believe in herself. I can't believe she's living her life the way she felt would be pleasing to others. It hurts to know that all these years she needed my help and I didn't realize it.

Why didn't she asked for my help? I thought we were the type of friends who could come to one another in time of need. Now that I know I'm going to do all that I can to help her build up her self-worth. How could I not know, it is amazing how you can be friends with someone and not know who he or she really is?

Paige was there bright and earlier ready for work. She was looking good on the outside but I know deep down her inside was full of self-doubt. I made her my new administrator. The timing was so perfect because my old administrator had given me her two weeks' notice. She was moving to LA to go after her dream as an actress. She worked with Paige her last two weeks. Paige caught on real fast and you can tell that her inside started feeling like she was looking on the outside.

We started looking for wedding locations and dresses. I started seeing a side of Paige that I had never seen before. I think this was the real Paige. After all these years I finally saw the real Paige.

Expecting

Tracie

I haven't spoken to Mike since that night. I still can't fathom how we ended up having sex. I must admit that it brought back some old memories but it wasn't the same. Mark and I have officially started dating, seeing Mike again brought closure to our relationship and now I feel okay with having another one. I never thought that I would fall for someone else besides Mike but being with Mark has changed my mind. I must admit he came across like a stalker, but once I got to know him he turned out to be a sweetheart.

He knows how to cater to his woman. He makes me feel special and loved. I can't stop thinking about him. I really believe that he will be the one I'm going to be with for the rest of my life. I just hope he find a career, because getting into the entertainment business can be hard. I'm not trying to take care of my king, he needs to take care of his queen. Oh well I'll cross that bridge when it gets here.

My stomach is starting to hurt again. This has been going on for the past few weeks. My body has been tired and my head has been hurting. I hope I'm not coming down with the flu. Mark has been coming over and fixing me soup and making sure I drink plenty of fluids. If this don't clear up soon I'm going to make an appointment to see the doctor.

I guess I should lie down, maybe I should eat something. I haven't eaten anything today. That's probably why my head is hurting. Let me hurry up before Mark gets here. I know he's going to be mad if he finds out that I haven't eaten.

On my way to the kitchen the doorbell rang and it's Irene. I haven't seen her in a while.

"Hey, Irene, where have you been hiding?" I asked.

"Nowhere," she said. "I just came by because I haven't seen you at Bible study lately."

"Yeah. I haven't been feeling too well. I don't know what's wrong. If it doesn't get any better I'm going to go to the doctor."

"What are the symptoms?"

"It seems like it's the flu. I get hot flashes, my stomach and head hurts."

"Are you pregnant?"

"Pregnant, no I can't be pregnant."

"The only way you can be sure of that is if you haven't had sex. So are you sure?"

I got real quiet. I really don't want this lady all in my bedroom business. And she's one of those old saints that don't believe in sex before marriage. I know if I tell her she's going to push me straight down the altar. I looked her in her eyes and said, "I'm sure I'm not pregnant."

"Well, honey, that's good to know. Just keep me posted and call me sometimes and let me know how things are going. You've gotten on your feet and forgot all about Ms. Irene."

"No I haven't, this job has been keeping me busy and my mother always needs me to do this and that for her. I can barely get any sleep."

"I do understand."

She gave me a hug and walked out the door. Pregnant, Lord, knows I can't be pregnant. I never thought I would get pregnant and not know who the father was. I'm not pregnant. Wait a minute did I get my cycle, where is my calendar I know I marked it and I just can't remember. I opened up my calendar and sure enough no mark. Maybe I'm late. Yeah, that's what it is. I'm late. I think I'm going to go get a pregnancy test just in case. I started counting back the days to see if I could determine around what time it could have been. I'm hoping that I was pregnant before I had sex with Mike. If telling Sade about what happened between us didn't stop the wedding I know this would and I don't want that to happen. Mike is a good man and I do not want to be the reason for messing up something that could be the best thing that ever happened to him.

I grabbed my keys and my purse and was on my way out the door. When I opened it Mark was standing there in the knocking position.

"Where are you on your way to?" he asked.

"I have to run to the store and pick up something real quick."

"Oh, baby, I will go for you. I know you haven't been feeling too well and you need your rest."

"I can do it, I need to get out of this place and get some fresh air anyway."

"Well, at least you can let me take you."

He's not going to let me get out of here alone. "Okay, baby," I said. We got into the car and my mind was going in circles wondering how I am going to get this test without him seeing it. I know men don't like buying feminine products so I can tell him that I'm going into the store to get that and I know he's not going to want to go in there with me.

We got to the store and sure enough he asked if I wanted him to go in there and get what I needed. I told him that I had to get some feminine products and I preferred to get them myself because I used a certain kind. He looked at me and said, "Cool I'll stay in the car. Do you mind getting me a pint of ice cream?"

"Sure, baby, is there anything else you would like for me to get?" I asked.

He said, "No," and I walked into the store. As I was walking down the aisle my mind went back to Jewels and when I found out that I was pregnant with her. Back then I didn't want to be pregnant because I wasn't ready for a baby and now I don't want to be because I wouldn't know who the father was. I grabbed the test, a box of panty liners, his ice cream, and walked up to the counter. I asked the lady to put the ice cream in a separate sack because I didn't want to have to open the sack until I got home.

I got into the car and he drove off. He looked at me and said, "You're so beautiful. I could spend the rest of my life with you."

In my mind I was thinking if you only knew what's going on at this moment with me you wouldn't be saying those words. I smile and said, "Oh really."

"Yes really. Ever since the day I met you you've kept it real. Your honesty blows my mind and your personality keeps me going."

Tears wanted to flow down my face but I did everything I could to make them stop. I leaned over, gave him a kiss, and said, "You're wonderful. I really didn't think I would fall for you but I have, and to hear you say those words helps validate my feelings for you."

We pulled into the parking space at the apartment, he opened my door, and grabbed my hand to help me out of the car. He asked me if I have eaten anything and I said, "No."

At that moment his attitude changed.

"Why haven't you eaten? Haven't I told you about going all day without eating anything? Don't you want to get well?"

"Mark, don't get mad. I was about to eat and then Irene came over. After she left I realized that I had to go to the store and now we're here."

"You're going to make me move in if you don't start taking better care of yourself. You go ahead and take care of what you have to do in the bathroom and I will whip up something real quick."

How did he know that I had to go to the bathroom and take care of some business? Oh yea, I did tell him I had to go get some products. I pulled out the box and began reading it. I don't know why I'm reading it because I already know what to do.

May hands are shaking. Okay, I did it. Now I have to wait two minutes. It's starting to turn. Okay we're looking good, it looks like a minus sign. No, what are you doing? I don't want that other line. No, not the other line. It's a plus. This can't be happening to me. I have to go and get another test. They say those thirteen-dollar ones don't always work properly. I'm going to go to the doctor. At least if it's true they will be able to tell me how many weeks I am. I put my evidence back in the bag and stuffed it under the sink. I'm not ready to talk about this right now. I must wait and see what the doctor say.

I walked out of the bathroom and into the kitchen.

"So is everything okay?" he asked.

"Yes."

"Well, you didn't have much of a selection. We should have gone grocery shopping while we were at the store. So here's some noodles."

"Oh thanks. I've been so busy and drained that I haven't had the chance to go to the store."

"Well I will go for you so when you get a chance write a list down and I will take care of it." He kissed me on my forehead and asked if there was anything else that I needed for him to do and I said, "No." He walked out saying that he will be back. He said something about a business meeting he had to go to. What am I going to do? Why am I always getting trapped in crazy situations? I grabbed the phone and dialed my doctor's office so I could schedule an appointment.

"Dr. Hopkins office, how may I help you?"

"Yes, my name is Tracie and I need to schedule an appointment."

"Have you seen Dr. Hopkins before?"

"Yes."

"What are you seeing her for?"

"I think I'm pregnant."

"How soon do you want to come?"

"Does she have any openings for today?"

"She's working out of the hospital today and I do show that she has one spot left."

"What time is that for?"

"At three, will you be able to make it?"

"Yes, thanks."

"Dr. Hopkins will see you at three. Please remember that she's working out of the hospital today."

"Okay thanks."

Let me hurry up and get on the road. The hospital is about thirty minutes away. I rather be there early than late. I can't believe this is happening. I finished eating the noodles, took a couple of spoonful of his ice cream, and ran out the door.

When I got to the hospital the parking lot was so full and the time was ticking. Finally someone was pulling out. I swooped in and ran out. When I got in there I noticed the time was different. I walked up to the receptionist and asked her what time it was and she said, "Two." Then she looked at me and said, "You forgot that time went back an hour." I smiled and walked toward Dr. Hopkins's office. Here I am, an hour early.

As I was walking down the hall I heard this deep voice calling my name. I turned around and it was Daddy walking down the hall-way. I walked up to him and asked, "What happened to your face?"

"Your daughter did this to me."

I couldn't believe it. She gave him a good beating. His lip looked like he had to get stitches and his left eyebrow had a big gash across it. I began to apologize but he stopped me.

"I'm the one who should be apologizing," he said. "When I met you, you had this beautiful glow about you. Your soul was full of peace and I envied that. I never had peace in my life and I thought that if I took it from you then I would feel better but I didn't. No matter what I did to you I still felt the same. Jewels woke me up. I had to sit in the hospital for two weeks. The last week a new nurse came in and she had that same glow that you had when I first saw you. She started talking to me about God and how He turned her life around. She told me that she had a pimp who used to beat on her and when she couldn't take anymore she ended up killing him. I know if it wasn't for the other girl, that your daughter was with, I really believe that she would have killed me. I felt the pain and anger come out in every blow and I deserved it. I wanted to say that I'm so sorry for causing you so much pain during that time in your life."

"I accept your apology. I know that it took a lot from you to make that step. I will let Jewels know."

"I wrote her a letter. I kept it with me because I didn't know when I was going to run into you. Please give it to her."

"I will."

He gave me the letter and as he was walking off I said, "Nothing is impossible if you believe." I got to Dr. Hopkins's office and signed in. I sat down and started thinking about what Daddy had said. I wondered if that same light he saw in me is the same light that Mark sees. I hope I'm not pregnant and if I am, I hope it's not Mike's. Five minutes later the nurse called my name. She weighed me and told me to pee in the cup. I was so nervous. Here I am peeing in this cup and if the result of this urine test comes back positive my whole life will change forever.

I went into the room and waited for the doctor. There was a knock on the door and I said, "Come in."

"Hi, Tracie, how are you doing today?" she asked.

"I'm fine."

"So I see someone thinks they're pregnant."

"Yep. I haven't been feeling well for the past couple of weeks."

"Well, let's see what the results are."

She opened up the folder and looked at me and said, "Someone is expecting a new baby."

My mouth dropped. This is not happening.

"Well, are you okay?" she asked.

"Yeah, I guess. I just wasn't expecting for you to say those words."

"If you're not doing anything to prevent yourself from getting pregnant then you should expect it, so do you want to start your prenatal care?" she asked.

"Yeah."

"Do you know when your last menstrual cycle was?"

"No, I'm not for sure."

"Let set an appointment for you to come back in three weeks. At that time we can do a Pap smear and sonogram to see how far a long you are."

"Okay," I said and walked out of her office. What am I going to do? It sucks not knowing who your baby's daddy is. At least I have it narrowed down to two men. I wonder if I should keep it. I mean who would know but my doctor and me. I can't kill an innocent child. What if God created the baby for a reason? I picked up the phone and called Mike.

"Hello."

"Hey, Mike, how are you doing?"

"I'm fine, who is this?"

"This is Tracie."

"Oh hey, Tracie, you want to speak with Jewels?"

"I called to speak with you. Have you been feeling a little tired lately?"

"No, why?"

"Well, I found out that I was pregnant and I was trying to see if you had any symptoms like you did when I was pregnant with Jewels."

"No, I haven't. Was I the only one that you were having sex with?"

"Why you all in my business like that?"

"You're the one calling me trying to see if I've been having symptoms. Now that gives me the right to ask questions."

"No, you were not the only one that I've had sex with."

"Tracie, I don't think this one is mine. I mean with Jewels I could tell right off the bat, I had more of the symptoms than you. You might want to check with the other man you're sleeping with."

"You're right. Tell Jewels that I will call her back later. I have to figure this one out."

"Hey, let me know, because if I am the father I will have to let Sade know."

"I don't want to mess up what you and Sade have. I would prefer you not to know so you won't feel obligated to tell her."

"Tracie, you can't call me with this kind of news and expect for me not to want to know the end result. You already know how I am about mine."

"Okay, let me call you back."

"All right."

He doesn't have the symptoms so he might not be the father. I wonder if Mark knows something and that's why he keeps getting on me about not eating. I don't know. I'm going to play it by ear.

I walked into my apartment and before I was able to sit down there was a knock on the door. I opened it and it was Mark. "Hey, baby, how are you doing?" he asked.

"I'm fine," I answered.

"So, where have you been? I came by to check on you and you weren't here."

"You know when I told you I had to go to the store."

"Yeah."

"Well, I went and got a pregnancy test."

"Oh really and."

"And I'm pregnant."

"I know."

"What do you mean you know?"

"At first, I didn't know what was going on with me. I started feeling tired and then one morning I woke up sick. Like a big baby I called my mom hoping she would know what was going on with me and she asked me if I'd gotten someone pregnant. I was like, "No, Mom, that couldn't be it."

She said, "Well, that's what it sounds like." And then when you told me you hadn't been feeling well I knew my mom was right."

"Why didn't you say anything?"

"I wanted to wait until you told me."

"Oh, now that's why you keep getting on me about me not eating."

"Yes and I was about to explode."

"So are you happy?" I asked.

"Am I, of course I am? I've already been shopping."

"Shopping with what money? I thought you didn't have a job."

"I've been lying to you about my occupation. I am in the entertainment business. In fact, I'm the CEO of Spanky Entertainments. I didn't want to tell you because I wanted you to fall in love with me not for my money. I felt bad having you pay for our dinner dates and movies. You don't have to worry about that any more. I know that you are down with me no matter what."

"You know you owe me, right? I was giving you my last."

"I know and I'm going to pay you back right now."

He reaches in his pocket and pulls out this ring. I never saw a diamond this big before in my life. I thought the ring that Mike gave me was big but that is nothing compared to this. He looked at me, smiled and then asked me if I would be his wife. I couldn't believe it. I took a deep breath and said, "Yes. Yes, I will be your wife." He grabbed me and started hugging on me. I pulled him back and said, "Before we go any further, I want you to know that my ex was here about a month ago for his uncle's funeral and we had sex. I don't want to start this engagement without being honest with you. I didn't tell you at first because I wasn't for sure if we were going to be serious and since we are I feel the need to tell you."

"What was done then is in the past. Today is when the commitment begins. You belong to me and I belong to you. I meant what I said in the car. You are the one that I want to spend the rest of my life with. I love you."

We laid down and cuddled the rest of the night, tears of joy fell from my eyes. I never thought that I could ever be loved like this again. I really didn't think that I deserved a second chance and now that I have it I'm going to cherish every moment of it.

Starting Over

Mike

I am so glad that baby wasn't mine. I didn't know how I was going to tell Sade if Tracie would have come back and told me the baby was mine. You don't know how hard it was to get Sade to answer the phone. She is one independent sister who is strong at what she believes. And when I finally got her to talk to me Tracie had the nerve to call me with that. I fell down on my knees and asked the Lord why? Why me, Lord? What did a brother do?

I didn't realize how much I was used to her being around until she was gone. When she opened the door I couldn't do anything but smile. She was looking good and I had to have her. Before I knew it I grabbed her and started kissing her. I picked her up and took her into the room. I felt like a dope head trying to get a hit. I was used to having sex every day and when she left it stopped. Not having that woman in my world for three weeks was hard. But that night was wonderful. I felt refreshed and energized. I went to work with a smile on my face. Everyone was looking at me wondering what was going on. Man I was so happy I let everyone leave earlier. I couldn't think straight because I kept thinking about last night. I thank God for Sade. I can honestly say that she is my helpmate. I wasn't this excited about marriage when I married Tracie.

She wanted me to go with her to pick out the wedding cake and photographer. I said, "Sure, baby." Any other time I would have come up with some excuse. She wouldn't let me go with her to pick out her dress. She said something about its bad luck.

I can tell that Jewels is trying to accept her. For some reason she thinks that her mom and I are getting back together. I want to tell her so bad that her mother has found her someone else and she's happy, but I'm going to let Tracie do that.

Jewels went with Sade and her friend to pick out dresses and she told me that it was fun. She talked about Sade's friend Paige. She was telling me how crazy and cool she was. She couldn't see how they could be friends because they're so different. I told her that opposites attract and that's why I like Sade because she's different from the ladies that I've been with.

She asked me again if I loved Sade more than I loved her mother. I didn't know what to say at first because I knew whatever I said it wasn't what she wanted to hear. So I told her that I love them both but in a different way. I knew she wanted more but I left it at that and walked out.

Sade and I scheduled the wedding for April of next year. I got my boys together and I know they were planning something crazy and wild for my bachelor party. I told them that I wanted something simple but I know simple is not in their plans.

We had our engagement party and that's when I finally met Paige, and Jewels was right she is different than Sade. I introduced her to one of my buddies and I think they hit it off real well. I noticed they were together the whole night after that. Sade told me that she was trying to find a nice man for Paige and I beat her to it. I was just trying to make sure that she had someone else to call besides Sade. I know how some single women can be and I've heard some of the things they say to their married friends.

My life is starting over and I'm loving every moment of it. I have a new house, new wife to be, and a beautiful daughter that I adore very much. Two years ago I wouldn't have thought my life would be this way and I thank God for the change. I can honestly say that He knows what we need better than we do.

Part of Life

Jewels

My dad told me that my mother called so I called her to see what was going on. Some man picked up the phone and at first I thought I had the wrong number and then he asked if I was looking for Tracie. I said, "Yes," and he gave her the phone.

"Hello this is Tracie," she said.

"Hey, Mother, how are you doing?"

"I'm fine, baby. Did your daddy tell you that I called?"

"Yep, who was that guy who answered the phone?"

"Oh that's Mark. I was calling you to let you know that I'm engaged and you're going to have a little brother or sister."

"What, Momma, you're pregnant? I thought you and Dad was getting back together."

"No, Sweetie, what your father and I had is over. We have gone on with our lives. He's with Sade and now I'm with Mark. You have to meet him. He's one of the nicest people you would ever know."

"I don't know, Momma, things are not turning out the way I thought they would. I thought you and Dad were going to get back together and we were going to be a family like we used too."

"You have two families now, Jewels. You have one here in LA and another one there in Dallas. Always know that your father and I will love you the same no matter who come into our lives."

"You're right. So you're pregnant? Wow, I'm going to be a big sister. How many months are you?"

"I'm not sure. I'll go back to the doctor in a couple of weeks and she will let me know then."

"I'm so happy for you. I can't wait to see you get big."

"I will keep you posted. If you come for the summer you will get to meet Mark as well."

"That would be nice. I will talk to my daddy about me coming."

"Okay."

"I have to get ready for school. I will talk to you later."

"I love you, Jewels."

"I love you, too, Momma."

My mother is pregnant and she has a new friend in her life. All this time I thought things were going to go back to the way they used to be. I guess it's not all about how I want it. I guess I have to get used to Sade. She's not that bad of a person. I really haven't given her the chance that she deserves. She hasn't done anything to make me hate her. Now that I know that there is no chance of my dad and my mother getting back together I might as well do like my mom said and grab hold of both worlds and pull out all the good I can. There is a knock at my door.

"Come in," I said.

"Hey, Daddy, what's up?"

"Nothing, you have mail, it looks like it's from LA. Maybe your mother sent you a letter."

"I just got off the phone with her. She didn't say anything about a letter. She told me that she was pregnant and that she's engaged."

"Oh really," he said. "So how do you feel about that?"

"I don't know. I really thought you two would get back together and we would be a family like old times."

"With time there comes changes. We all expect things to turn out a certain way but in the end it's better than what we could imagine."

"She wants me to come to LA and visit her this summer."

"Well, that's cool. You need to spend more time with her and grab hold of some good memories."

"I wonder who this Mark person is."

"It's kind of funny how you are okay with your mother having a new friend, but you weren't with my friend."

"Because I thought there was hope. Now that both of you have someone else I know there's no hope for the two of you getting back together."

"Everything happens for a reason. I still love your mother for who she is and what she brought to my life. If it wasn't for her I wouldn't have you."

"Oh, Daddy."

"You're my angel and I love you so much. I really hope that you and Sade can become friends. She is a really nice person and she likes you a lot."

"She was real nice to me while you were gone. It was cool hanging out with her. I think I will give her a chance."

"I think that would be a good idea."

"Well, let me read what my mother wrote."

"Is that your way of telling me to get out of your room?"

"Daddy."

"Alright I'm gone."

I wonder why my mother didn't tell me she sent me a letter. I opened it and it reads:

Hey, Jewels,

I ran into Daddy and you beat him up pretty bad. Anyway he was telling me how sorry he was and that he wanted to give you a letter that he wrote. I've enclosed the letter. I didn't read it, Lord knows I wanted to. Call me if you want to talk about it.

Dang, I must have been really mad. I wonder what he has to say. I opened the letter and began to read:

Sorry that I don't remember your name but I wanted to say that I'm sorry. I know that what I did was really bad and

166

I deserved every punch you gave me. I know that these words can't take away the discomfort and hurt that I caused but I just wanted you to know that I was wrong for what I did and I'm sorry.

From Runny Jr (aka Daddy)

I wonder what made him write this letter. Why? Wasn't telling my mother enough? I still can't believe that I beat him up the way I did. I'm just glad that no one else will get hurt by him anymore. I appreciate him coming forward and admitting he was wrong. I know that had to take a lot of courage.

I don't know what to think or say at this point. So many life-turning things have happened to me in the last couple of years. My mom and dad are divorced and have found them someone else to spend their life with. I'm going to have a new stepmother and stepfather plus a little sister or brother. Natalie has turned her life around and is back at home with her family. She found her a boyfriend who loves her for who she is and not her body. Troy and I still communicate from time to time but the feelings are no longer there. We both realize that we're not the same people that we were when we first met. We agreed that we would be better off being friends. I guess my true love will find me one day, but until then I will continue to find out who Jewels really is and what I really want. I can truly say that none of this was in my plans. Oh well, I guess all of this is a part of life and all I can do is live every moment of it as if it was my last.

About the Author

Mrs. LaKisha Avery-Stewart, a native of Texas, has been writing since she was in middle school. Her writing started with poetry, then plays, and now books. Mrs. Avery-Stewart always had a passion for writing and acting. If she is not writing or acting, you can find her sitting in her director's chair. When it comes to writing, she likes to write about things that will touch the souls of all ages. She finds the most challenging part of writing is ending the story. Her advice for writers young and old is to never give up on allowing God to use you in one of the most creative way possible. In her free time, LaKisha spends it with her family. She is married with four kids: two boys and two girls. Being in the Christian setting not only gave LaKisha the faith to continue on this journey but the courage as well. With that in mind, she knows in her heart that with God, nothing is impossible, and he is the one that is directing her path. Keep your eyes open and your ears clean because Mrs. Avery-Stewart is on fire pursuing her dreams.

CPSIA information can be obtained
at www.ICGtesting.com
Printed in the USA
FSHW020744120820
72878FS